EXTENDING *Your* HERITAGE

This book was created as an outreach of the Heritage Builders™ Association—a network of families and churches committed to passing a strong heritage to the next generation. Designed to motivate and assist families as they become intentional about the heritage-passing process, these resources draw upon the collective wisdom of parents, grandparents, church leaders, and family life experts, in an effort to provide balanced, biblical parenting advice along with effective, practical tools for family living.

For more information, write, phone, or visit our Web site:
Heritage Builders™ Association
c/o Chariot Victor Publishing   1-800-528-9489
4050 Lee Vance View   www.faithparenting.com
Colorado Springs, CO 80918   www.heritagebuilders.com

The Heritage Builders™ resources include:

Your Heritage: A foundational book explaining the Heritage Builders™ ministry's key concepts. (Trade paper)

Family Night Tool Chest books

An Introduction to Family Nights   Basic Christian Beliefs
Bible Stories for Preschoolers, OT   Bible Stories for Preschoolers, NT
Christian Character Qualities   Holiday Family Nights
Money Matters Family Nights   Proverbs Family Nights
Simple Science Family Nights   Ten Commandments Family Nights
Wisdom Life Skills   Ready for Adolescence (Coming soon)

Family Fragrance: Filled with ways to develop and create an AROMA of love in your home. (Trade paper)

Extending Your Heritage: Shows how the Heritage Builders™ concepts can be used by extended family and other concerned adults to pass on a spiritual legacy to children. (Trade paper)

Family Traditions: Filled with ways to celebrate old traditions and mark spiritual milestones in your family. (Trade paper)

The Family Compass: Practical help for parents as you point your child's spiritual compass toward God. (Trade paper)

Heritage Builders™ Curriculum: A small group adult study focusing on the importance of establishing and passing on a family spiritual heritage. (Thirteen-week curriculum)

These resources from Cook Communications Ministries are available through your local Christian bookstore.

EXTENDING *Your* HERITAGE

J. OTIS LEDBETTER
& RANDY SCOTT

Cook Communications

Faith Parenting is an imprint of
Cook Communications Ministries, Colorado Springs, Colorado 80918
Cook Communications, Paris, Ontario
Kingsway Communications, Eastbourne, England

EXTENDING YOUR HERITAGE
© 2000 by J. Otis Ledbetter and Randy Scott. All rights reserved.

Printed in the United States of America.

2 3 4 5 6 7 8 9 10 Printing/Year 04 03 02 01 00

All Scripture quotations, unless otherwise indicated, are taken from
the *Holy Bible: New International Version®*. Copyright © 1973, 1978, 1984
International Bible Society. Used by permission of Zondervan
Publishing House. All right reserved. Scripture quotations marked KJV
are taken from the *King James Version.*

Contributing Editor: Gary Wilde
Editor: Julie Smith
Cover Design: Koechel Peterson
Interior Design: Pat Miller

Library of Congress Cataloging-in-Publication Data

Ledbetter, J. Otis
   Extending your heritage/J. Otis Ledbetter and Randy Scott.
      p. cm.
   At head of title: Heritage Builders.
   Includes bibliographical references (p.) and index.
   ISBN 1-56476-783-3
      1. Church work with children. 2. Church work with youth. 3.
   Evangelistic work. I. Scott, Randy. II. Heritage Builders
   Association. III. Title.

BV1475.2 L37 2000
259'.2--dc21   99-059257

No part of this book may be reproduced in any form without written
permission from the publisher, except in the case of brief quotations in
articles or critical reviews. For more information, write Cook
Communications Ministries, 4050 Lee Vance View, Colorado Springs,
Colorado 80918.

Table of Contents

Dedication

To my first granddaughters:
Riley Nicole
and
Madalyn Rose
I promise you my watchfulness
and
Dedicate myself
to help you know my Great God
and
His character.
J.O.L.

To BJ, my wife, my friend, and the mother of our children
If it were not for your encouragement,
there is much in my life I never would have attempted,
including this book.
R.S.

Acknowledgments

To those who have contributed to this work through our surveys and by sharing their stories, we say thank you.

To our friends and fellow board members of the Heritage Builders Association, who have held in trust the "Will of the Vision" to the Heritage passing process, the pages of this book could not accommodate the words of our appreciation.

To my wife, Gail, who started me on this journey three books ago and continues to be my fuel of encouragement. You are an awesome force to watch!

To pastors and teachers who daily stand up and give hope for the future. And to all who extend themselves beyond the call of duty and give selflessly to care for those who have no model to follow. If there was one, you would deserve a Nobel Prize for heritage passing.

To my assistant and friend, Sherry Krigbaum, who organizes my calendar, mitigates my mistakes, and continues to work tirelessly for me anyway. You are indispensable. I hope you don't read this page and find that out.

J. Otis Ledbetter

I would like to thank Kurt Bruner, Jim Weidmann, and J. Otis Ledbetter, the founders of the Heritage Builders Ministry, for sharing with me the Heritage Builders concept and including me in this wonderful ministry. The way I approach my responsibility to my children and the children of others will never be the same.

Randy Scott

Introduction

*O*h, please God, no!" shouted Martha, as her right foot slammed on the brakes of her '84 Chevy pickup. Her voice was quivering from surprise by the event unfolding in front of her. Tired from previously driving, her husband Ray had just nodded off and the events of the moment jolted him awake in time to witness the horror.

It was a dangerous thing they did, stopping on a two-lane highway on a cold, black night. But not stopping would have been worse.

What Ray and his wife had observed was a car pulling back onto the highway from a natural trench that paralleled the roadway. Running behind the car in the ditch was a small child trying to catch up with the vehicle. They couldn't tell if it was a boy or a girl. Ray's first instinct was to chase the car and catch the perpetrator. He thought he had just witnessed a case of molestation.

"They could have a weapon in the car, or there could be more than one person in that car," he reasoned out loud. "Not only that, if we catch up with the car, the tables might be turned and we could find ourselves accused." Frantically he jumped out of the truck and ran around to the driver's side as his wife slid over to the passenger seat.

With all kinds of thoughts racing through his mind, the lights of the suspect car disappearing in the darkness, and the child in harm's way on a busy highway, he abandoned any plan of pursuit. Quickly he looked out the back window, searching for the child who had stopped running and was now lying in the ditch underneath a blanket. He found himself in a precarious position, pinched between oncoming traffic, a guard rail on his right, and eighteen-wheelers blowing past with horns blaring, narrowly missing his truck, on his left. The extreme danger was intensified by the sight of the blanket, now completely covering the child, rising and settling with each gust of wind created by the speeding trucks. The child was precariously close to the road.

Ray carefully backed his truck against traffic toward the ditch. When he got close, he jumped out of the truck and quickly headed toward the child. To his surprise, the child got up and ran toward him, leaping into his arms, holding on with all her might. The cold and the fear mixed to make her shiver in his arms.

"A little girl," he muttered under his breath.

"What's your name?" he asked.

"Buffie," came the reply.

"How old are you, Buffie?"

"I'm this many," she said, holding up three fingers.

He hurried to his truck and secured her in a seatbelt. He still had the urge to catch up with the car, and well . . . the human reaction was to make them pay. But instead, Ray turned his truck around and headed toward the nearest city to report the crime. Questions poured into Ray's and his wife's minds. Before they could ask them, the little girl spoke.

"I don't know why Mommy left me there," she mumbled with her head down.

Twirling the edge of the blanket between her thumb and fingers she looked up at Ray and said, "I guess it was because I was crying." By now the tears were flowing.

"Mommy said I was crying too much. I didn't think so, but I guess I was."

It wasn't an attempted molestation, he realized. It was an abandonment. "A mother," he swallowed hard, "abandoned her little girl."

An unusual story, for sure, and perhaps a bit too gut-wrenching for some. But when Ray was relating the story to me, it was a perfect opportunity to make a point. The events around that story make our emotions run deep and passionate. It strikes a discordant chord, shakes us up, makes us uneasy if not down-right angry, and calls us to some sort of action.

When I think of those who have had no role models in their homes to illustrate what a heritage is and how to extend it to the next generation, I get a similar feeling in my gut. It doesn't matter whether the abandonment was caused by death or some social collapse within the family. The void is there just the same. Like Ray, we have an urge to go after the perpetrator and do the natural human thing. But that does not rescue the victim. Besides, vengeance is not the intention. Rescue is, because many remain in the trenches, under cover, and hope for the best in a dangerous situation.

The need to connect with family and community remains great. Some find themselves searching for that connection. They look to jump into the arms of church, school, clubs, sports, neighborhoods, all kinds of situations to find a place where they connect best or belong most. Sadly some never find it—or find it in the wrong place, but others do make a connection. The good news is that there are people on both sides looking for someone with whom to connect: those needing to link who have had no role model, and those, thankfully, who long to share what they were given.

That is what our book is about. We hope that when you finish this book you will want to join the search. Our goal is that you will want to reach beyond your family. Whether you find yourself as a grandparent parenting again, a volunteer parent, or have the occasion to do some sidewalk parenting, we hope you will see the opportunities to influence a child with your values. We hope you will intentionally stop and make conversation with children and teens whether at a mall, church, school, or on your home street. We want to encourage you to be aware of the "least of these" as Jesus called them in Matthew chapter 25, in the busyness of your day, even if it takes risking, to build a bridge toward them so they may have an avenue to connect with Him through you.

If you are in search of a model or see yourself, as Buffie, having been abandoned for whatever reason, our desire for you is that you will be willing to receive from someone who is willing to give to others a heritage they did not receive.

If you have never reached out to another to give out of the abundance of your life, we pray you will open your heart wide enough to fit a child, teen, single adult, divorcee, or anyone in need into your world. Read on and understand the rationale behind *Extending Your Heritage;* then find out how to begin, enjoy some success stories from the Bible and corroboration from some contemporaries. Allow God to use you in a way perhaps you never dreamed, but others, even as we speak, are dreaming of.

J. Otis Ledbetter
Randy Scott

⤞ Chapter 1 ⤝

Restating the Heritage

The old, silver-haired man slowly stood. Trembling, he turned his back to the tombstone where he had been kneeling. Rising to stare his wife in the eyes, he wailed, "Tell me I've lived a good life." With his voice trailing off to a whisper, he forced the words out again. "Tell me I've lived a good life."

These words come from the last scene of the blockbuster movie *Saving Private Ryan*. The old man was reacting to a dying request made by a soldier assigned to rescue him. He was the sole survivor of five adult children. The war had cruelly taken the lives of his four brothers, and the war department was bent on not allowing the fifth son to fall victim. So the military sent a specially chosen group of men to the front lines to bring him out of harm's way. The commander of the group, having been shot and knowing he wouldn't make it, left a dying request for Private Ryan to see that he made his life count.

Kneeling at the commander's grave on the cliffs of Normandy almost fifty years later, Private Ryan wanted someone to tell him that his life was worth the sacrifice those soldiers had made for him.

I could not hold back the tears. His remark hit the bull's-eye of my heart as it did for many sitting near me in the theater. After all, isn't that the wish for most everyone: that our lives count for the good of something or someone?

> **PRINCIPLE**: To realize the importance of receiving and living a heritage that counts to the good of something or someone.

> **INTENTIONAL IMPACT**: Understanding the value of extending the heritage to others and to the next generation.

A Basic Instinct

Call it whatever you want, inside each of us is a deep desire to know our past and influence our future. The desire seems to intensify with age. It's as if we live the first forty years of our lives looking forward to what we want to be and what we want to accomplish; we look forward to the future to influence the future. Then slowly, we turn 180 degrees during the next few years. We now find ourselves looking back over our lives . . . to influence the future. The realization that we have lived a legacy and are leaving a heritage now stares us square in the face.

It is a basic instinct given to us all. The great and wise Solomon, moved by the Holy Spirit, wrote in his journal called Ecclesiastes that, "He [God] has also set eternity in the hearts of men; yet they cannot fathom what God has done from beginning to end" (Ecc. 3:11).

> **Generations at Church**
>
> . . . . .
>
> I had never seen three generations of a family attend the same church regularly until getting involved with our current church. It's great to know that's what I'm starting for our family with young children.
>
> *C.F. Ramsey, MN*
>
> . . . . .

Solomon is articulating a timeless truth. We sense that there is more to this life than just living and dying. Yet we can't comprehend the beginning of time, and we can't grasp that someday time will be no more. We find ourselves somewhere in-between. We long for connection. Where did we come from? Where are we going? Where do we fit into the great scheme of things?

Solomon's dad, King David, helped lighten the weight of those questions. He responded to life by saying to God, "From the ends of the earth I call to you, . . . I long to dwell in your tent forever. . . . For you have heard my vows, O God; you have given me the heritage of those who fear your name" (Ps. 61:2, 4-5).

The heritage!

What David said certainly connects him to the past, and those who gave him that heritage were connected to the future through him.

What Is a Heritage?

We all have received, are living, and are passing a heritage. David realized what he had received and from whom he received it. A heritage is:

> That spiritual, emotional, and social legacy passed from parent to child . . . good or bad.[1]

Why the spiritual, emotional, and social? This is what Jesus was growing through according to Luke 2:52: "And Jesus increased in wisdom and stature, and in favour with God and man" (KJV). Favor with God is His spiritual component, favor with man is His social element. Increasing in wisdom and stature, of course, are His physiological and mental capacities. Since everything that happens to us, whether physically or psychologically, is registered in and recalled through the memory of our emotions, we chose to use emotional as encompassing the last two components. Therefore, the heritage we received, are living out, and are passing to the next generation includes those three ambient factors.

Extending a Heritage

It is interesting that the description of Jesus' path to adulthood included these factors because these components are the same for everyone, not just God's Son. It is also noteworthy that Joseph was not Jesus' biological father. He was a stand-in for the Father. Joseph extended his heritage to a child who wasn't his. This child was put in Joseph's care to influence Him through His formative, growing years. The heritage Joseph received from his parents became a part of the heritage of the Father's Son.

All this brings to the forefront a wonderful opportunity that each of us may encounter during our lives. Prior to the announcement from an angel to him, Joseph was unaware that he would have the privilege of extending his human heritage to a child God put into his life intentionally and trusted him with explicitly. It is a wonderful moment when a couple has a child. The heritage process begins immediately. But isn't it also wonderful when God, unexpectedly, puts into our lives a child who isn't ours but is still someone He has given to us intentionally and trusts us with explicitly? That is what we call *extending your heritage*.

Extending your heritage is defined as:

The process of sharing your heritage with those who may not have a strong heritage of their own.

Who Can Extend Their Heritage?

Those who have discovered and mastered the art of giving a strong heritage should extend that blessing to others. It is a wonderful gift to be shared. It should not be stockpiled. The whole idea of a heritage culminates in the idea that it is given to be shared. The writer shouts the plan in Psalm 78:5-7.

> He decreed statutes for Jacob
> and established the law in Israel,
> which He commanded our forefathers
> to teach their children,
> so the next generation would know them,
> even the children yet to be born,
> and they in turn would tell their children.
> Then they would put their trust in God.

Perhaps the answer to the question "who can give an extended heritage?" is anyone, if they understand the process and they recognize and seize the opportunity. We have witnessed many who are products of an extended heritage. Some of their testimonies will be given throughout this book. They include parents, grandparents, aunts, uncles, childless couples, single adults, and teachers—anyone who knows what a heritage is and wants to extend that heritage past themselves into the lives of others.

Working for God

Dad demonstrated that in every job we need to work as for God. Our family cleaned our church for a number of years. We all hated bathroom duty, but many times Dad would volunteer to do this hated task. I can still hear him singing, "I come to clean the pots, I come to clean the pots. ..."

R.B. Morrisville, PA

Getting Started

As we travel the nation giving workshops, we are approached by those interested in sharing their heritage with others. If a person wants to extend her heritage past the immediate family unit, then an understanding of what a heritage is becomes necessary.

Kurt Bruner and I (J. Otis) wrote a book called *Your Heritage* in which we thoroughly explained the heritage-passing process. Randy and I can't fully cover all the information in that book here, but we do feel it necessary to restate the heritage in condensed form. After we give an overview of the heritage process, we will then speak of the importance of extending your heritage in community settings.

Threefold Cord _____

As we explain the following three components (spiritual, emotional, and social), keep in mind that they are really inseparable. Each legacy is dependent on the others for the strength of the heritage. We describe them as a braided cord. There is strength in the union of the braid. For instance, when a heavy enough weight is connected to one of the cords apart from the braid, it will break. When the braid is complete, each cord strengthens the other. A weight heavy enough to snap one of the cords by itself is easily carried by the braided cord. We can even use a pair of scissors to sever one cord inside the braid, and the support that the other two cords bring will still hold the heavy weight. We can even sever another cord a few inches down from the first break and the cord still has amazing capacity. The strength is in the union. Solomon points out this principle in Ecclesiastes 4:12 where he states "a cord of three strands is not quickly broken." The strength of the unbroken cords can then carry the weight of a heavy load that life may bring while the weakened cord is being repaired.

The beauty of extending your heritage to someone who has weaknesses in all three components of their heritage is that your heritage may be the very thing they need. The strength of your legacies can be what they require at that time to hang some heavy life circumstances on while their cord is in repair. Emotional strength, social connections, or spiritual insights you may possess and extend to them may make the difference in their decisions at a critical time in their life.

The Spiritual Factor

The most important part of an extended heritage is the spiritual component. It deals with the unseen realities of the spiritual life. In *Your Heritage*, we define this part of the heritage as:

The process whereby parents model and reinforce the unseen realities of the spiritual life.

We stress the importance of understanding that a spiritual legacy is not an event or a ceremony. It is a process, a long scriptural obedience moving in the same direction. It is more *caught* than *taught*. Henceforth, we reinforce precepts and principles through modeling the lifestyle.

Precepts are not necessarily learned by rote, but the principles that are prerequisite to the precepts of the extended spiritual heritage become a lifestyle. For instance, when driving through a school zone the precept might be painted on a sign that says, "25-mile-per-hour speed zone." The principle undergirding the precept is "drive safely" because the lives of children are at stake. We may not be able to repeat the words on the sign verbatim, but we know the principle without hesitation when nearing a schoolyard full of children. In the same manner, we may not know the exact wording of the ninth commandment, but we have its principle down pat: namely, that lying is not a good thing and will come back to bite. So, tell the truth!

Since we live our lives in the realm of the senses, we tend to equate reality with the physical. Those things we can experience with our five senses become to us the things that are actual. The truth is, the things we can see are temporal. The things we cannot see are eternal and are truly real and will last forever. Those are the things from above that our affections should be set upon, and not the things of the earth.

Joe's dad was a pastor who had a secret. He didn't reveal the subject of the family secret, he just called it the "family problem." It wasn't alcohol or substance abuse. Turned out it was numerous affairs. Joe lived with the problem until he could leave the nest. When he left he moved in with a friend, disclosed his father's lies, and left the faith. The shenanigans of his father surprisingly did not have visible affects on his social or emotional legacies. But the spiritual legacy his father passed to him was obviously flawed. Joe rejected it totally.

Joe eventually met a young lady, married her, and determined to forget the God of his father. That is, until he met a couple named Lyle and Mary. This couple invited the younger couple over for meals. They went to sporting events together and took special interest in the baby born to Joe and his wife. Joe and his wife even occasionally agreed to attend church with Lyle and Mary. For the first time, Joe witnessed genuine faith from a truly godly man and woman. Lyle and Mary became spiritual models for the young couple. Because of the strength of his and his young wife's emotional and social legacies, Joe was able to find a spiritual resolution with his God rather quickly. Oh, you should see them now. They have two children. Joe is in leadership in his church. All because an older couple decided to extend their heritage to help strengthen the weak spiritual legacy of a potentially embittered young man.

Humbled, yet thrilled about the results and the opportunity to extend their heritage, Lyle and Mary are looking for the next person God might send their way.

The Emotional Factor

The emotional legacy is a close second to the spiritual legacy in importance. Many are weak spiritually because of some emotional scar. Any kind of abuse will leave its deep mark. Some will live their lives ineffective spiritually because their past is littered with the debris of an abusive relationship with a parent, a close relative, or an authority figure.

A strong emotional legacy is defined as:

> That enduring sense of security and emotional stability, nurtured in an environment of safety and love.[2]

A strong emotional legacy will give us healthy emotions to help people deal in a positive way with the struggles of life. The strength of this legacy will enable the other two components of the heritage (spiritual and social) to flourish. On the flip side, a weak emotional legacy will cause the other two components to suffer.

When I was a youth pastor in Southern California, a young man I will call David began attending the class. David was a kid most teens shied away from because he was backward and a bit unkempt. His clothes were dowdy and his hair nappy and long. David asked that I not come by his house, and I tried to honor his request. I sensed something askew but never got the opportunity to talk to him about it at church. David rarely missed the Sunday Bible class, but there was one stretch of Sundays that he failed to attend. I didn't want him to slip through the cracks, so I decided to drive to his house to see if I could be of any assistance. I found David sitting

.....

Day-to-Day Christian

My grandmother was such a day-to-day Christian. She didn't lecture about her faith. She lived it quietly, which made the boldest statement. Many Wednesday evenings my grandparents would pick me up, and my grandmother always had a hot meal ready for me in the backseat. On the way to church I would eat and they would tell me stories of when they grew up.
B.P., N. Richland Hills, TX

.....

on the couch in the living room of his parents' dilapidated house. He came to the door to greet me. I could tell immediately that something was drastically wrong. He led me around the side of the house and began to relate the story he had been hiding for so long. David's mom was chronically ill. When his dad couldn't handle the thought of his wife's pain, he retreated into alcohol and anger to hide his disappointment with life.

The condition of the house reflected the lack of care that permeated the entire atmosphere surrounding the family. The liquor intensified his dad's anger and he took it out on David. He asked me to follow him to the garage. There he showed something to me that I hope I never see again. Attached to the rafters was a chain. David pulled back the cuffs of his shirt and showed me chain marks on his wrists.

"When Dad is in a rage; when he can't take the fact of Mom's constant illness," pausing, he finished his sentence, "this is where he brings me to punish me."

David was taking the punishment for his mother being sick. I felt sick to my stomach.

My wife and I helped remove David from that situation, but the emotional scars seemed to always be there in every decision to distract and confuse him. The abuse destabilized him. Socially he was a dwarf, and spiritually he constantly struggled with the thought that a Heavenly Father could love him unconditionally. We helped get him into a situation where people extended their heritage to him. The strength of their legacies gave David a place to rest and repair his emotional wounds. The last time we saw him he looked optimistic and healthy.

The atmosphere surrounding our lives emotionally should warm the heart, not tighten the stomach. One of the greatest statements concerning an emotional legacy is made by Jesus when He invites all to "come to me, all you who are weary and burdened, and I will give you rest" (Matt. 11:28).

Jesus creates a place of emotional stability and security for each person that is nurtured in an environment of His safety and unconditional love. That is a perfect model for every heritage extender to imitate.

The Social Factor

The social legacy is the core of people relationships. It is:

giving the child the insight and strong social skills for cultivating healthy, stable relationships.[3]

To some that is downright frightening because we realize there are gaps, for some even gaping holes, in our social heritage extending efforts. I encounter many moms and dads when I speak at conferences and retreats who are close to panic in this area. Just this past summer while speaking at a men's retreat in the mountains of Southern California, a gentleman told me that during his pursuit of economic status, he failed to prepare his son socially. "I think I did okay with the spiritual and emotional components," he boasted. "Home was a safe, restful place, and my church has helped in the spiritual training." Then he lowered his chin and said, "But . . . I failed to take the time to teach my son about people and choosing friends."

I don't know if I was much consolation trying to help him find solutions to rectify his son's bad choices of friends, but the man was sincerely grieved at the gaps in this part of the heritage he was passing.

When Joanna's father took his last breath and passed away I was beside his bed with her. Joanna didn't even cry. Later her aunt confided in me that Joanna suffered slight autism. The autism wasn't severe enough to be detected immediately. But this condition rendered Joanna socially inept and caused trouble with her relationships. Aunt Effie was now Joanna's only living relative and she lived more than eight hundred miles away.

I was pleasantly surprised when a lady from our church took Joanna under her wing. Judy hired Joanna as a partner in her cleaning business. During working hours Judy teaches her about social skills. The two are connected, and Joanna is making strides in her social graces.

Just a few weeks ago I learned that Joanna's aunt is not expected to live much longer. I looked toward heaven with a thumbs-up gesture and thanked God for Judy and her extended heritage to Joanna!

Whether gaps happen accidentally or intentionally doesn't matter. The fact is, gaps are there. It becomes a challenge to finish well and perhaps repair the breaches of social unity and community found in the heritage we have been extending.

Community Living _____

Rugged individualism is a romantic idea, but is it reality? Yes, we are to be individuals. Yes, each is unique. Like one mom jokingly tells her three children, "Each of you is unique, just like all the rest." But aren't we given a responsibility to be in unity or community with our individualism? Just because we are individuals each created unique by God doesn't give us license to be loners. It doesn't mean we can soak up life and never give out. If good values are to be extended to the next generation, if Psalm 78:5-7 is to be realized, then in our individualism we need to connect with others and reproduce those values in them and in the next generation. That puts us into a community of people. In that community there are those who need help in the weaknesses of their legacies.

Paul told the members of the church at Phillipi to "do nothing out of selfish ambition or vain conceit, but in humility consider others better than yourselves. Each of you should look not only to your own interests, but also to the interests of others" (Phil. 2:3-4). This appears to be an extension of the passion of

Christ when He prayed to the Father for His disciples, "so that they may be one as we are one" (John 17:11b). Each chosen disciple was unique in his personality and gifts, but one within the community of Jesus' followers. Jesus, in extending His heritage to these men, was affirming that, indeed, the disciples would need each other and that they should operate as one.

This is true of the secular realm as well as the spiritual. A businessman needs customers, a teacher needs students, a coach needs a team, an author needs readers, and vice versa. Neither can function successfully in their capacities without the other. Within that specific community of doing business they become interdependent. They need each other. Life is made to function this way.

When one is socially inept within his or her world, the function of these concepts becomes flawed, and unity or community begins to break down.

Two Enemies of the Extended Community

When extending your heritage there are some enemies of community and extending a heritage that we all need to be aware of. These enemies are called misrepresentation and manipulation. They should be uncovered and exposed before moving on in the extending process. These identifiable enemies slither their way into people's social lives. At first, a child or teen looks good, and perhaps reasonable, to a heritage extender because he seems to be an instant connector. But if these enemies are present in the child, they have the potential to bite like a viper. Be careful how you step around them.

Misrepresentation: Webster, in his first edition,1828 dictionary, says this is "giving false or erroneous representation, either maliciously, ignorantly, or carelessly."[4] It is information injected into the mix of living with the intent to mislead for gain. These misrepresentations usually seem harmless, and probably are when done ignorantly or even carelessly. When used as an instrument for gaining some advantage, misrepresentation becomes a mean tool against social unity. It eventually alienates the user. A person will resort to it when she feels a need for her status to be upgraded, perhaps not knowing that the use of it only puts her more on the "outs" socially.

Eric, a young man to whom a teacher in our Christian school was extending his heritage, seemed addicted to this enemy. He told stories of how great he skied, or how he told off a teacher, even how he once had a car similar to or better than the one anyone else had. Now, he wasn't outright lying. He did ski, he did have a confrontation with a teacher, and he did have a car. But when the kids went skiing, when the truth was known about the confrontation, and when everyone saw his car, most everything he represented was laughable. So, Eric, who didn't measure up to his own press, felt a need to continue to misrepresent. As he did, he continued to lose social station with his peers.

Granted, people sometimes harmlessly exaggerate. A savvy person will calmly catch it early and counter. Sometimes in the ministry we call it "ministerially speaking." A nice costume to cloak a false outcome.

Manipulation: According to Webster's 1828, this word comes from a root word that means to "work by hand."[5] Newer dictionaries add to the definition saying it means to "manage or to control artfully or by shrewd use of influence, often in an unfair or fraudulent way." The 1828 edition does not mention the latter. The original definition leads me to conclude intent is involved. When one works a work with his hands, there is design and meaning to his efforts. Manipulation has those components. There is always intent and design inherent within its framework.

A young girl to whom my wife, Gail, and I tried extending a part of our heritage could be the poster child for manipulation. If a manual is to be written for it, I want to be her agent. If this child would put as much effort into schoolwork as she does into designing her manipulation of the system, surely she would be wealthy. She knows the angles, she is aware of all loopholes, and she has a backup to her backup plan. She knows how to introduce so much information into a plot to manipulate it that everyone's head is swimming—except hers.

Even though it has a mostly negative connotation, all manipulation isn't necessarily bad. Negotiation is a form of manipulation. When exercised within the bounds of decent behavior it becomes an effective tool in doing business. I always enjoyed watching my kids try to "work" mom or dad. Of course, Gail and I were aware that we were being manipulated, so we would use the occasion to counter selfish orchestration and try to turn it into negotiations.

When our children would try to work one parent against the other, we created a rule. For instance, the kids would plan an overnight visit by a friend. Knowing their chances were better if they could use a little manipulation, they would wait until Gail and I were in different places, then ask one of us to okay their plan. If the answer wasn't satisfactory, there was always the other parent who had not yet heard the first answer. Before parents get a chance to communicate on the issue, sometimes this can work well to a child or teen's advantage.

Gail and I got our heads together and drafted a plan. Whichever parent made a decision first, was the decision we all lived with. We also addressed the issue of bringing the friend with them to ask us, thinking this tactic put pressure on the affirmative side. Not so! A simple rule took care of that: Ask in front of a friend and the answer is an automatic, "No!"

With these simple ways, we tried to quietly teach them the

difference between negotiation and manipulation. We knew that the realization of the difference was a mechanism they would need in future social relationships, whether friendships, business, marriage, or parenting.

We bring up the issue of these enemies because in our experience of extending our heritage, those who are not serious have fooled Gail and me. They wanted the connection as a means to climb a social ladder, borrow some money, get a date with our son or daughter, or other elements of our family that they could take some advantage of. Extending your heritage takes risk indeed, but there is a myriad of people out there who are earnestly yearning for connection. Cull out the counterfeits and get to the authentics. Guaranteed, they are out there waiting for someone to extend their heritage to them.

Putting It All Together _____

I was eating dinner at a men's retreat in Big Bear, California when the chair next to me was quickly occupied by a nervous gentleman. With six other men at the table, he seemed reluctant to ask a question. He started and stopped several times. After his many failed attempts to say something, I looked at his nametag and blurted out, "Max, what is it exactly you want to ask?"

His ruddy complexion turned a deeper red. As if he were wading through a slough, he began, "I'm fifty-eight years old."

Long pause.

"I still live with my mother, b-b-b-because she's not well."

By now the entire group at the table was silent, listening for the question. Max kept plodding.

"I'm single, I have no children, have never been married, and don't have any plans to be."

Then came the crux of the problem that had been gnawing at him through the first two sessions of the retreat.

"So . . . what does a heritage have to do with me?"

He drew a deep breath, raised his fork, took a bite of his potato salad, and finished the question with a bulge in his jaw.

"And what do I have to do with it?"

I just love to be asked that kind of a question with an audience. Nobody else got to say anything at the table for the rest of the evening, because I expounded on the extended heritage. All were nodding their heads in affirmation as I spoke to Max. What you have just read in the previous pages is the essence of what I covered in the two sessions previous to Max's question. What you will read in the remainder of this book is how his question was answered.

It was with pleasure that I saw him connect to the information I gave him and leave the table that evening with a smile and a mission on his mind. At the three sessions the next day, I saw Max writing furiously. Even now I wonder how he is implementing what he soaked in that weekend.

→ Chapter 2 ←

Yearning for Connection

We are a nation of "to and fro-ers." We hurry from place to place, filling up our lives with sports and occupational stimuli, sometimes over-scheduling ourselves and even, at times, our families. In the hustle and bustle of the every-dayness of life, what do we have that can really sustain us? What can sustain us emotionally? What can undergird us spiritually and socially?

We believe it is connectedness. The feeling that we are a part of something larger than we are that gives meaning to life and to ourselves.

PRINCIPLE: Our very life depends on being connected to something bigger than ourselves.

INTENTIONAL IMPACT: To help identify places where connection may take place, so we may affect and nurture those connections.

Contacts and Channels _____

It is necessary to understand that connectedness doesn't mean contact. We are in contact with people all the time. We see them at the local high school football game, we encounter them at the grocery store or in the neighborhood fast food establishment. Usually the contact begins with a "Wow, haven't seen you lately," or a "How've you been?" question that means nothing more than a casual "hello," as we anxiously push our carts loaded with merchandise toward a packed checkout stand. And those casual contacts usually end with a nonchalant "See you around," or "Catch you later."

If contact alone was the important issue here we would be overwhelmed with it. Our lives have so many contacts we sometimes feel like the beautiful flower wanting to rise toward the sunlight but find ourselves choked out by the overgrowth of vines in the flower bed. Vines like overcommitment, time constraints, or a lack of confidence in our social skills get in our way.

We also should not equate connectedness with channels. As intriguing and helpful as the internet may be, it does not compensate for connection. We chat with people living on the other side of the world. We "instant message" our acquaintances through online service channels, sometimes having four at a time on our computer screen while trying to keep up with the subject matter from each. We are channeled but not connected. Not the kind of connections that are life changing. Sure, contacts and channels are valuable to a salesperson, but is a Rolodex full of names and addresses that valuable to a person who finds himself alone in the crowd?

> · · · · ·
>
> ## We're Watching
>
> I remember my dad telling some of my younger aunts and uncles that "You need to stay clean" because his daughters were watching. And we were! Because my aunts and uncles stayed virgins until marriage it stressed the importance of this for me and helped me face the world's pressure to have premarital sex.
>
> *R.B. Morrisville, PA*
>
> · · · · ·

There is good news. The kind of connection we are yearning for is available. But it is important that we understand the meaning and value of being connected with someone. Some say our life depends on it.

Connections Matter

Dr. Lisa Berkman, now chair of the Department of Health and Social Behavior at the Harvard School of Public Health, published a ground-breaking study in 1979. An accompanying book hit store shelves in 1983.

The study followed the lives of about seven thousand people in Alameda County, California. The study lasted for a nine-year period. To measure the effect of the study, Dr. Berkman's team surveyed people to find out if they were connected or not connected. They found out whether the people were married, lived alone, and what kind of contact they had with friends or relatives. Did they work with volunteer organizations, and were they involved in church or civic fraternities?

With this information in hand, Dr. Berkman's team looked at the people's risk of dying over that nine-year period. Was there proof of increased or decreased risk of ill health to those who were disconnected from extended family, friends, or community ties?

She found that the most isolated people were three times more likely to die than those with strong connected ties.[1] This was one of the first proven tests that social isolation and lack of connection has been tied to death.

In his book *Connect*, author Edward Hallowell, MD writes:

> *Life is loss. For all we gain we also lose—a friend, a day, a chance, finally life itself. To oppose the pain of loss, we use a human glue, the force of love. The force of love creates our many different connections. This is what saves us all. If you*

think about what you live for, what really matters to you, you usually think of some person or group of people. . . .

These are all different kinds of connections. To thrive indeed just to survive, we need warm-hearted contact with other people. The close-to-the-vest standoffish lifestyle is bad for your body and soul. Like a vitamin deficiency, a human contact deficiency weakens the body, the mind, and the spirit. Its ravages can be severe (depression, physical illness, early death) or they can be as mild as (underachievement, fatigue, loneliness), but they are certain to set in.[2]

The key to gaining the benefits of connections is to have many kinds. Your church family, close relatives and friends, or volunteer organizations are examples of places to connect. It might be in these places where a person can best choose another with whom to extend her heritage, but certainly there are many who are isolated outside organizations such as these. They are the ones who need someone to say, "Here, I will help you get what you did not receive." Just as in Dr. Berkman's survey, the people in most danger of dying were the ones most isolated; when thinking of extending your heritage, the ones most isolated are the ones most in need.

Extending your Heritage to your Family . . . and Beyond

Though many mentoring organizations make an effort to connect children to someone outside their immediate family, we think there are times when a reconnection to family can be a healthy situation. We hear stories of twins separated at birth or within their preschool years who later yearn to find that other person. Some will even hire an agency to find the lost sibling. We've witnessed long-lost brothers and sisters coming together after forty or fifty years apart. I (J. Otis) have helped parent and child come back together after one began to live a lifestyle that was not acceptable to the other, but over the course of years the separation was too great a pain and they reconnected.

One familiar example from Scripture is the Prodigal. Another personal example is a fellow named Jack who left the East Coast thirty years ago and moved to California because of political differences with his family. So great were the differences that there was no communication between them. Those differences don't seem so great anymore. The thirty years have healed the wounds. Jack told me a few months ago that he was going back to see everyone, and he was nervous. He is going to reconnect with the family he abandoned nearly one-third of a century ago.

A Personal Example

I turned my face to the wall, away from my roommates, because the tears wouldn't hold back. Even though the room was dark and both roommates were asleep, I didn't want them to awaken to the sound of my nose sniffing. I wasn't hurt. No one had been mean to me. I wasn't short of money, nor was disaster ready to strike. It now seems childish and I am a little embarrassed to talk about it, but I was simply disconnected. I was loosed from family for the first time in my life and I

. . . . .

Sunday Lunch

When I was a kid I looked forward to monthly after-church luncheons served on the church grounds. This wasn't our regular church, but our neighbors knew how much I enjoyed coming, so we were always invited. I learned about food and fellowship and how all the members of the church contribute for a common good. It taught me why we are called to meet together as one body.

B.P., N. Richland Hills, TX

. . . . .

didn't like it. College life was new and different. Acceptance was now conditional, in fact I found myself having to prove my worth again and again to every new person I met. And at college one meets tons of new people. It was a phase that was short in duration, but it was real and a bit frightening to this young boy of seventeen.

Now I know some will think that is laughable. I understand, because in hindsight so do I. I well remember how being under the rules of the family seemed suffocating. At times I resented the controls. I couldn't wait to get out from under Mom and Dad's authority. I couldn't wait for big brother to disappear. It all seemed so exciting.

That time finally came. My 1956 baby blue Ford was packed to the gills. The tank was full of fourteen-cents-a-gallon gasoline and the nose of that vehicle was pointed north of Sherman, Texas, headed toward Springfield, Missouri. I couldn't have been happier. I couldn't have felt freer. I was my own man and my wings protruding from my back were beginning to stretch and unfold. Feathers were all over my car! I had all the answers; I was ready to make my mark on this world. A mark that everything at home kept me from making.

Sound familiar?

The tears didn't come at first. It took a couple months. What I was experiencing didn't feel like loss, it felt more like freedom. It then began to dawn on me that what I had had was what I was yearning for again . . . a feeling of connection that family gave to me. It was that yearning that caused the chasm and brought the tears.

I never really lost my family connection during those few short months at the beginning of college life. I just perceived it that way. But that yearning taught me I needed to work toward being connected wherever I was placed.

A Key to Connection

The loss of connection is not singular to today's culture. It isn't a feeling of loss because of the absence of material things. Perhaps it's more a loss of family identity. As parents, we sometimes feel at a loss as to how to fulfill this yearning we find in our children, so we tend to do nothing. Think how those without a parent or parents feel. This longing for connection cannot be overstated because it is so closely tied to who we are.

In his booklet *A Parent's Guide to a Christian Bar Mitzvah*, Craig Hill writes about connections. He calls them blessings and cursings.

> *When we are talking about blessing and cursing, we are not talking about flattery and profanity. We are rather talking about God's impartation and Satan's impartation of identity and destiny in people's lives. Identity is simply the answer to the question, "Who am I? Who is this 'me' that I must live with each day?" Destiny is the answer to the question, "Why am I here? What is my purpose?" Either God or Satan can answer these questions in each of our hearts. However, neither God nor Satan tends to impart messages of identity or destiny directly, but rather operates through human agency.*
>
> *As a matter of fact, God was so concerned that each of us receive His impartation rather than the devil's that He placed His agents in each of our lives to ensure that this would happen.*
>
> *These agents are called parents. If parents do nothing else on this earth regarding their children, the one thing God intended for them to do is to make sure that they are agents of God's impartation of identity and destiny to their children and not agents of Satan's impartation.[3]*

It is a basic need of every person regardless of age, station, or culture. If you find a child or teen yearning for this type of connection, and they have no parents to fill the role of that God given agency, stay tuned. We have some valuable information to share. We want to help you fulfill their yearning by exposing you to some different types of connections we call repeat parenting, neighborhood parenting, and sidewalk parenting. And if you find yourself disconnected, don't despair. You have a lot of company with people who found a way. What they lost, they regained. Two such examples from the scriptures are an apostle named Paul, and a governor named Joseph. One is outside of family, the other is within the family.

Paul

We are not told a lot about the family life of the Apostle Paul. We are given modest insight into his life by a few mentions of his education, Gamaliel (his professor), and his former occupation. His immediate family connections are hidden from readers for whatever reason. We are, though, given quite a good look at his personal life. His emotions float to the surface on certain occasions. Several hold particular interest to me. His relationship to young Timothy, whom he calls his son in the ministry, is especially intriguing. This is the only time he seems to mention family, and this is beyond immediate, to extended family. Paul has taken the position of a father to Timothy. It was important enough to be recorded in God's eternal Word. Paul has chosen to pass the blessing of his heritage to Timothy.

Paul also wears his emotions on his sleeve when he writes to his beloved friends in the church at Phillipi. He longs for them (Phil. 1:8). He *epipotheo* for them, a Greek word meaning to earnestly yearn, to intensely crave. He invokes God as his witness to his longing. It's as strong a statement as could be made. Connection is important to Paul. He yearns for it. The path of his life is a lonely one and he too, like us, looks forward to the feeling of belonging.

Joseph

Joseph, in the book of Genesis, has long been known for his integrity and loyalty. Yes, he shook off the seduction of a powerful woman, endured prison as an innocent man wrongly accused, and forgave those who used him for their personal gain. Each incident is a story of its own, indeed, but the part where he yearns for family connection has taken a backseat.

Forced into slavery and separated from family, Joseph found himself a missing person. He was a boy who had a strong faith in the Word of his God and believed without a reason to believe. He had a fire within him. A fire that told him he was special. Then without a trace he disappeared as into the night. His dad was told wild animals had eaten Joseph.

Wade through all the stories about Joseph from Genesis chapter thirty-seven to forty-two: his dad favored him, his brothers hated him for it; he was sold into slavery; he was falsely accused of rape; thrown into prison and forgotten. Then spend time from chapters forty-two through forty-eight: he was brought out of prison to interpret Pharaoh's dreams; he was exalted in Egypt's kingdom to second in command; he had a chance to impact his family; he rejoiced in God's deliverance. Through all of this, you can sense the strong emotions that come out of the desire to be reconnected.

Satisfying the Yearning

It is not our intent to say that the yearning alone is reason to reach out to just anyone. There is a vulnerability that needs to be dealt with first that comes with the territory. There is a responsibility that also comes with it, and the last thing disconnected people need is to experience rejection again, even if it is from well-meaning people.

Both Joseph and Paul left us a guide to connecting or reconnecting to family and extending our influence beyond. They tiptoed slowly through the process and left some very clear tracks. When looking for someone to extend our heritage to, instead of jumping in with both feet, perhaps we might follow their footprints:

He recognized the need.
He evaluated the circumstance.
He counted the cost.
He proved the people involved.
He risked reaching out.
He made the connection.

Recognize the Need

The desire to connect was inside Joseph but didn't show itself until his brothers exposed their need. Immediately he surveyed their situation and knew he could reach into his lost family and meet the need. He wanted desperately to reconnect with his family. By doing so he not only was responsible for saving his family, but he extended his new heritage to an entire nation.

Paul, who had no children of his own, recognized the need of a struggling young Timothy and reached beyond his family to be a father figure to him. (If Timothy had the influence of a father it isn't mentioned. Only his mother and grandmother are named.)

It won't take long for a need to surface if we have the yearning to connect beyond our families. The needs are all around us. One does not have to go looking for them; they will find us. It might be you will recognize the need through a casual

. . . . .

Treasures at Church

Smiles, hugs, and prayers are the things I treasure most about my church family.
K.P. Pleasant View, TN

. . . . .

contact. Maybe it's a boy or girl who attends your church. You've even heard him say things like "I would like to go, but there is no one to take me to the youth activity," or you observe her sitting alone Sunday after Sunday and your heart goes out to her loneliness. Maybe you see a child short on social graces, or in a situation similar to one in my church where a young lady abused by her father had no idea how to dress—to coordinate colors or style. She was someone you couldn't help but notice. A woman in the church connected with her and taught her those graces. Someone recognized the need and now the two are inseparable. They even work together. What a difference!

There is a famine in our land, and it is not necessarily a famine of food. It is a famine of meaningful, healthy relationships. A drought of community ties that is creating hunger pangs for a genuine bonding.

Evaluate the Circumstance

Perhaps you're asking, "How do I know when it is the right person or the right time to extend my heritage? How do I evaluate the circumstances?"

Someone said that most folks ricochet through life. They bounce like a super ball from one circumstance to another, reacting to life instead of responding. Rarely do they stop to evaluate a circumstance so they can respond. Instead they create more havoc by their quick, sharp replies. If you find yourself doing that in a possible "extending your heritage" relationship, slow things down and evaluate the circumstances. Having done that, you may then learn to respond and create a path to connect beyond yourself into the life of someone who has a need. Otherwise you may never see the need even though the yearning is right in front of your eyes.

You have two options.
You can choose to respond, which is positive.
You can choose to react, which is negative.[4]
—Zig Ziglar

Joseph did not react. He responded. He could have reacted and blown the whole thing. He could have angered his brothers with vengeance, alienated them with his position, aggravated them with his games, or arrested them and held them as prisoners the rest of their lives for what they did to him, but he didn't. He chose to respond instead.

Not only to say the right thing in the right place, but far more difficult to leave unsaid the wrong thing at the tempting moment.[5]

—Author Unknown

When Jake and Beth were deciding whether to extend their heritage to Ronnie they had to evaluate several elements. Ronnie had been brought up on the streets and knew how to both misrepresent and manipulate situations. He had no role model but the law of the street. Ronnie had the potential to either turn into a talented young man or steal them blind. He had spurts of goodness. He had an innate ability to communicate.

The worst did happen. He stole from them. Instead of reacting and saying the wrong thing at the tempting moment, Jake and Beth chose to respond positively. They began to teach him the value of things. They taught him the worth of character. Their response paid off. Their evaluation allowed them to be ready for the worst if it happened. Their response made Ronnie respond. Even today they remain faithful to extending their heritage to this young man.

Count the Cost

Three areas of concern are laid bare here. There will be a cost to involvement in the lives of others. One will need to count the cost in these areas:

Time
Effort
Resources

Involvement to extend your legacy beyond the realm of your present status will mean adjusting your schedule to include the proper amount of time to accomplish your goal. It may mean attending sporting events or dance recitals for a child with no parental support. The amount of time you can afford will directly affect the depth of involvement you may want to give. That amount of time will determine the effort and the resources you make available.

Sixty-two-year-old Steve has decided to extend his heritage to the child of a single mother. The boy has no grandparents, so Steve is filling the void. Both love golfing. That costs time and resources. Steve knew it when he entered the relationship. "It was and still is worth it," says Steve.

Counting the cost cannot be overstated. If time is available and not much money, then plan things that cost little or that are free. If your energy level is low, plan events that aren't exhausting. Do things at home. Bake cookies, play table games, teach a home skill like quilting, sewing, painting, or woodworking. Not counting the cost in time, effort, and resources could wind up inadvertently hurting you and the one with whom you wish to share.

Prove the People Involved

What seems to the reader of Joseph's story an intricate game of cat and mouse is really a proving process. He needed the truth.

He set his brothers up to allow them to withhold it. They did not. He let the rope out a little to see if it would be jerked out of his hand. Would they come back if he let them go? After all, his previous encounter with them in the fields of his dad's domain was less than honest. They lied before, would they again? They stole before, would they again? He set out to prove their intentions concerning honesty and integrity. What a well-devised plan! Their true character should surface through it, and it did. Joseph felt free to take the next step.

Those we seek to bring into our heritage should also be proved. Not, perhaps, in such an elaborate plan, but their intentions validated just the same. Are they truly in need? Is there a void in their life that can't be filled any other way? What is their need and am I equipped to meet it?

Terri and Paul tried to help Kathy by extending their heritage to her, but Kathy's emotional problems surpassed the ability of Paul and Terri to meet them. Alcoholic parents had raised Kathy, which taught Kathy to be the ultimate excuse maker. What Terri and Paul offered wasn't a good enough crutch for her. Kathy wanted someone to agree with her that she didn't need professional help. She seemed to be looking for more excuses for bad behavior. The relationship was hurt by unmet expectations. The couple expected Kathy to respond to their offerings. She didn't. Kathy expected the couple to swallow lame excuses. They didn't. The proving process part of the relationship ended the project. Terri and Paul were looking for someone to extend their heritage to, but Kathy was looking for someone to manipulate.

As stated in chapter one, there are enemies to the social legacy you intend to pass. Again, those enemies called misrepresentation and manipulation should be weeded out before you take the next step.

Risk Reaching Out _____

Risk! What a scary word! Just saying it brings reluctance to the forefront of any venture. It connotes the possibility of loss to the risk taker. But there has to be a measure of risk in every relationship or it may never grow.

Jesus told a parable of three men who were given talents. To one the master gave five talents. To another he gave two, and to the other he gave one. His instructions to them were to take care of his property. The one with five doubled, as did the one with two. They were honored on the master's return as good and faithful servants and given more. The man with one talent buried it to keep it safe and returned only one upon the master's arrival. He was called a slothful and wicked servant.

Wow! Why? He worried over the one talent. He didn't lose it. It was intact and well cared for. Yet he was chewed out big time. The reason? He was afraid of his master so he refused to risk.

Thirty-eight-year-old Jill told me she wanted to reach out to Sherri, an elementary school girl in her neighborhood. Sherri had no mother, and Jill was fearful the single dad would take it wrong and think she was coming on to him. To start and not finish because of a possible misunderstanding would be unfair to Sherri. Jill was afraid of failure.

Grandparents have said they want to reach out to their grandchildren, but the relationship with their own children makes them fearful of doing it.

Fear is not a reason for not reaching out. To reach, you must risk! To risk you must overcome fear. The "junk yard dog" of fear guards the road to our pool of potential. We must distract it—if not slay it—to reach our full potential. So after recognizing the need, evaluating the circumstances, counting the cost, and proving the people, take a risk. . . . It's time to destroy fear.

Make the Connection

Oh, how Joseph connected! He showed himself to his brothers. He wept in front of them. He forgave. He threw a feast. He sent for his father. He went before Pharaoh and asked for land for his family. He went all out so all could feel and witness the connection.

When you decide to take the risk and make the connection, it will be one of the biggest thrills you will experience. You have decided to share your heritage with someone who wasn't given one. You may be responsible for beginning the generational blessing to a whole new family. What a gift! What a beautiful satisfaction to the yearning for connection.

Connecting Dots and Building Bridges

As a child, one of the games we played in the car or at restaurants, was "connect the dots." Mom had them available to keep our short attention span in check. It was always fun.

All that is visible when the game begins is numbers and black dots. Follow the numbers beside the dots in order, and a picture emerges. At first its shape is unclear. Then when the one dot is connected that makes the puzzle take shape, a shriek of excitement tells everyone you've figured it out. You simply follow the plan until the picture is complete. Go where you want, forget the numbers, and you have a mess. Nothing resembling a picture.

The process of passing a heritage is not exactly as easy as connecting numbered dots. But there is a framework that one can follow to establish a heritage of your own and then extend it to others. Heritage extending is a process. So the framework establishes the starting point, then one continues to follow the plan.

In chapter one, the heritage was restated. The starting point is the realization that you are passing a heritage good or bad. Then, there are tools whereby you can improve and further the process. By using the tools and staying with the process you are on the way to getting and giving a heritage. Once that has been put in place, perhaps you are now prepared to extend it beyond your immediate family.

Let's have some fun. Don't look at the following list and be overwhelmed. We are not asking you to take all these steps at once. That could be depressing. Only let it serve as an object lesson to what extending your heritage is like over a period of time. We created a dot and numbers picture for you, and the dots in the following order stand for a process that ideally could end in creating a beautiful picture of what you are accomplishing. Indulge us and have fun allowing the picture to emerge as you follow the plan.

1. Realizing your heritage
2. Evaluating your heritage
3. The spiritual legacy
4. The emotional legacy
5. The social legacy
6. Planning your heritage-passing process
7. Using the family fragrance tools
8. Using the family compass tools
9. Using the family traditions tools
10. Learning how to extend your heritage
11. Recognizing the need
12. Evaluating the circumstances
13. Counting the cost
14. Proving the people involved
15. Risking reaching out
16. Making the connection
17. Starting the process all over again

Bridges

"What's a child's game doing in a book designed for adults?" you may ask. At least I hope you ask, because my answer depends on the question being asked.

Every time you think of the "connect the dots" game, we want you to think of connecting with a child or teen who needs your influence. Every time you see a bridge, we want that bridge to remind you of a person who needs a bridge built to him. A person who does not have a heritage being passed to him. We want you to consider evaluating him. We want you to consider taking the risk and reaching out to him. After you have selected the child or teen, then let's consider the type of bridge you will build toward him or her and begin to plan.

⇢ Chapter 3 ⇠

Being a Heritage Extender

∽◌∽◌∽

I (Randy) have often thought back to my fourth grade teacher, Mr. Pappas. What a special person, a man who made learning great fun for children. I remember one particularly creative method for cajoling us kids into doing more reading. He signed us up for a reading club that would deliver books to us all through the year. Then he held a contest, announcing, "Everybody who reads all the books, and turns in all their reports, gets to go to the circus!"

He knew the Ringling Brothers were coming to town, and he told us all about it. Regularly!

Throughout the year we kids could hardly contain ourselves with anticipation. And I don't remember any classmate who wasn't sitting in the crowd with me on that happy spring day—eyes bulging as shaggy lions jumped through hoops and muscle-bound young men flew through the air.

Why Reach Out?

One way or the other, Mr. Pappas made sure that every one of his students succeeded. He always gave all he could to us. He was always willing to stay after school to help tutor us and then give us a ride home so our parents wouldn't have to be inconvenienced.

> • • • • •
>
> ### Live Like Jesus Lived
>
> My family was blessed by a couple who treated people with respect and love. It did not matter if you were rich or poor, elderly, or a child. Everyone was welcomed in their home. They seldom preached God, they just lived like Jesus lived.
>
> *R.B., Morrisville, PA*
>
> • • • • •

Did you ever have a Mr. Pappas in your life? The message of this book is that we need more Mr. and Mrs. Pappases in our midst today. There are at least two powerful reasons why: the challenge of our downward-spiraling society, and the clear call of the Scriptures.

PRINCIPLE: Children and teens have major negative influences speaking to them in many venues that someone needs to counter.

INTENTIONAL IMPACT: I will search, find, and expose the negative influence, then perform my responsibility to extend my influence into the next generation.

Today's World Challenges Us: Invest in Youth

Children are being powerfully influenced today by a questionable set of values that daily comes hurtling at them full speed. Just consider the influence of television, the movies, the media, child-oriented media, and even the public schools. Not all of it is good, clean fun.

Rather, our children are bombarded with post-modern views that are quite confusing, especially when compared with what they may hear at home or in church. It's certainly much harder to live in a world where there is seemingly no right or wrong. In such an environment, how do I know if I'm succeeding or failing? In this era of "enlightenment," it's more important than ever that we, as Christians who've been graced with a strong moral heritage, find creative and inspiring ways to pass it on to the next generation.

In the previous chapters, we've talked about the social, emotional, and spiritual legacy we want to leave to the next generation. We realize that we ourselves were powerfully influenced by others in our growing-up process. We can point to strong mentors who took us under their wings and showed us how to live as good citizens and growing Christians. During those precious times we matured and grew socially, emotionally, and spiritually. But we can't just hoard that blessing. We can't be content to savor it for ourselves. There comes a time when it is our turn—our opportunity to be torchbearers for the next generation. In this day and age, it's probably more important than ever that we extend our heritage, not only with our immediate family, but by reaching out to those we come in touch with throughout our lives.

The bottom line is that our children and young adults long for mentors and heroes to emulate. I came across a statement in a Christian magazine that brought this theme home for me:

Americans are living in a post-heroic age, where young adults are much less likely than their parents to have national role models. A survey by Scripps Howard News Service and Ohio University shows that 60 percent of adults have no heroes. Of those who do have heroes, most said their heroes are either dead or are historical figures.

Defining "hero" as anyone with admirable courage (other

*than family or biblical figures), the study revealed that the
last thirty or forty years has been a time of extreme cynicism
toward heroes, in which a media-wise culture has witnessed
the debunking and demythologizing of one so-called hero after
another. It's not a healthy trend. . . .[1]*

The trend must be reversed. And it's our turn to try.

We ourselves have been the benefactors of "heroes" invest-
ing in us throughout our youth. We have now reached a certain
maturity level. Those of us who have raised our children and
helped them on their way have accumulated the invaluable
experiences of life, and now it is time for us to give back by
helping that next generation grow up. Because the world we
live in is so dangerous to the souls of our youth, we need to
come alongside this next generation, with great caring and
encouragement, and show them the way to go. Even the Bible
tells us to do it.

The Bible Tells Us: Care for the Next Generation _____

Just take a moment to consider the overall testimony of the
Scriptures. This idea of generation-to-generation transmission of
a heritage resounds as a basic principle all through its pages. In
virtually every portion of the Bible you see it. Here are just a
few examples:

*Be careful, and watch yourselves closely so that you do not
forget the things your eyes have seen or let them slip from
your heart as long as you live. Teach them to your children
and to their children after them (Deut. 4:9).*

*Tell ye your children of it, and let your children tell their chil-
dren, and their children another generation (Joel 1:3 KJV).*

Things we have heard and known,

things our fathers have told us.
We will not hide them from their children;
we will tell the next generation
the praiseworthy deeds of the Lord,
his power, and the wonders he has done.
He decreed statutes for Jacob
and established the law in Israel,
which he commanded our forefathers
to teach their children,
so the next generation would know them,
even the children yet to be born,
and they in turn would tell their children.
Then they would put their trust in God
and would not forget his deeds
but would keep his commands (Ps. 78:3-7).

He took a little child and had him stand among them. Taking
him in his arms, he said to them, "Whoever welcomes one of
these little children in my name welcomes me" (Mark 9:36-37a).

You then, my son, be strong in the grace that is in Christ
Jesus. And the things you have heard me say in the presence
of many witnesses entrust to reliable men who will also be
qualified to teach others (2 Tim. 2:1-2).

Why not take some time to meditate carefully on these and similar passages? We're sure you'll be reminded of other instances in the Bible in which the people were called to remember the blessings of the Lord and to convey them to the next generation. That was constantly the case in the Torah. And then the prophets, like Joel, warned that even God's judgments must not be forgotten. This is eloquently echoed by the psalmist: never attempt to hide God's deeds from children, grandchildren, or great grandchildren.

Then, in the Gospels, Jesus himself showed us how important

Christian Holiday Traditions

My parents and relatives decided to place an importance on Christian holidays even when my grandparents weren't Christians. Other family members, as well as myself, reached out in a nonthreatening, caring way to help them get to know Jesus Christ.

K.P., Pleasant View, TN

the younger generation is by making a truly amazing pronouncement: when you welcome children, you welcome Jesus. I think about that sometimes when I watch the children's workers in my church teaching the little ones to sing and quote memory verses. What a blessing to be doing these things directly for Jesus! Finally, in the Epistles, we see the Apostle Paul calling a young man his son. What a close bond he'd developed with Timothy, sharing with him "all about [his] teaching, [his] way of life, [his] purpose, faith, patience, love, endurance" (2 Tim. 3:10). Here was a case of a seasoned Christian taking a young man under his wings to mentor him in the things of God—and of life, in general.

We can do this, too. But we need to know how.

How do we reach children? How do we come alongside of them? How do we position ourselves to make an impact? It's not easy, but it's certainly not impossible. We suggest taking these four steps:

First, Find Out What Kids Want and Need

Many communities are using a program called Assets for Youth. It's geared around giving kids what they need to succeed. It asks tough questions like, "Why do some kids handle growing up with ease, while others struggle?" "Why do some kids avoid dangerous activities while others get involved in all kinds of risky behaviors?" "What causes one young person to beat the odds while another continues to remain trapped?"

Of course, many factors influence why some young people enjoy success and others seem to have a harder time. However, research by The Search Institute has identified specific practical things that can have a positive and lasting impact on youth. Rather than focusing on problems, this research concentrates on the developmental assets—the positive things (like parent support and commitment to education) that help young people thrive. Such research is, of course, "market driven." That means it starts with the wants and needs of its "target client." So . . . have you thought about the wants and needs of kids lately? Consider:

1. Kids want unconditional love and a feeling of connection. Most kids feel they must earn their parents' love. Today's baby boomer parents are the ultimate achievers, which has resulted in a generation of kids who feel emotionally abandoned by adults. Kids want better communication with their parents and with adults, but parents are often too busy to move beneath the superficial. The fact is, kids desperately want more time with their parents. We recently ran across some statistics saying that the average mother spends about two hours per week in meaningful discussion with her child. A dad spends about one hour. Many parents think "quality time" is more important than quantity. But the reality of it is, kids long for the quantity.

2. Kids need a clear and compelling sense of purpose in life. A recent survey showed that many kids believe all religious faiths are basically the same, and they tend to reject the paths their parents have taken. Because of a lack of a sense of direction, and this feeling of not sensing a purpose coming through spiritual means, kids are taking anywhere from five to seven years to get through college. Yes, in this generation too, young adults are still trying to "find themselves." Suicide rates are up, and young adults bounce from job to job as they seek their special place in society.

3. Kids need greater acceptance of their friends by parents. Kids today are very relationship oriented. When we accost their friends, or talk about their friends in demeaning ways, it poses a great challenge to their loyalties. But why force your children to choose between you and and their friends? Make time for having their friends in your home. Feed them. Sit down and ask some questions that show your genuine interest in them. Today's teens, especially, can engage you in some fascinating conversations. Have you tried it?

4. Kids want a deeper emotional closeness among all family members. Are you surprised by this? Maybe you've tried to talk to your teenager recently, and all you get in return are the standard three responses: "Huh? Yeah. Nah." But be assured, your kids want to be able to relate to you in a way that shows they're capable of genuine emotion and caring. But are we building those close-knit bonds in our families? Are we willing to speak with children about the depth of our love? Can they do the same. In some families, it's possible. Actor Jeff Bridges said of his famous father:

> *My dad, Lloyd, taught me about acting. He wasn't pushy, but whenever there was a part for a kid on his TV show* Sea Hunt, *he got me or my brother, Beau, into it. Even when I was only eight, he'd sit me down and teach me the basics.*
>
> *With my dad I feel as though we're in the same race, and he's passing the baton. It sounds corny, but if we were sitting alone, it wouldn't be unusual for me to talk about how much I love him.*
>
> *I feel my family is on the same team, rooting for one another. Having that kind of love and support has given me a real responsibility. It's the responsibility of being blessed and not squandering it.2*

Kids yearn for a deeper respect and closeness between their

parents too. How often do they fail to see our talked values modeled by our acted values? For example, they want less financial stress within their families. They sometimes wonder if their parents are even capable of handling money, as so much emphasis (and argument) relates to the financial standing of the family. Such constant wrangling creates insecurity. Yet with what is blaring constantly in the news, with school shootings, dire stock market predictions, and global hot spots, the world is becoming a truly scary place. Kids yearn for a place where they can feel safe.

Second, Show You Care _____

Once you have a sense of what kids want and need, you can begin to show your concern. You show your caring not by the gifts you give, but by the time you invest. You see, there's a great chasm between adults and children today, particularly between adults and teens. Our youth feel abandoned, and they feel that adults are afraid of them. One contributing factor is that we adults tend to cocoon. Nowadays in many households both husband and wife work, and when they come home, they want to draw the blinds, turn on the TV, and plop on the couch. Don't bother me, kid!

This goes directly against one of the key assets identified in the research we mentioned above. For a child to grow up and become a successful member of society, he or she needs an environment where adults are acknowledging kids. As we read more about this asset, we became more and more convicted. How could we begin to acknowledge the youth in our neighborhood?

I tried a little experiment involving the kids standing at the bus stop near my home. In the past, on every weekday morning as I pulled out of my driveway to head for work, I'd drive past ten or fifteen kids waiting at a bus stop. Naturally, I'd ignore them, and they would ignore me. To test the "acknowledging kids theory"

I'd been reading about, I decided to do something different one day. As I drove by the bus stop, I raised my hand and waved.

How shocking! Many of the kids were so surprised by my act that they didn't respond, although a couple of them did wave back. Each morning thereafter I continued to wave, and each morning more and more of the kids began to wave back. Now, I am pleased to say that after many weeks of this exercise, not only do the majority of the kids wave back, but as I bump into them in the neighborhood (no, not with my car!) they will smile and say, "Hi!"

Sounds like a pretty insignificant thing, right? But that proved to me the power of adults caring simply by acknowledging. Really, it's a small step, not difficult, but filled with potential.

Third, Keep Being Available _____

Caring assumes availability. Even though our lives are incredibly fast-paced and hectic, we can be on the lookout for kids in need. We can be ready to drop our agenda in deference to their agenda.

In chapter five of this book we will talk about being ready for "teachable moments." Those are the times in which, in the course of everyday living, we come across prime opportunities to make positive impact on a kid. We have to be ready, constantly vigilant for such a moment. When it comes, it may call for a powerful spoken word, a meaningful action, or a significant expression of sharing. Whatever it requires, the moment is precious and memorable. And we need to be there for it.

Being available simply means we're observing situations as they happen, waiting for the appropriate moment to lend an ear, a word, or a hand. That's exactly what happened to make an Olympic and professional champion out of a young man who could have gone in a totally opposite direction:

When I was a kid in Louisville, my parents gave me a brand new bicycle. Proud and happy, I parked it outside a gym one day. Then somebody stole it, and it just about broke my heart. Someone told me there was a policeman in the basement, and when I found him, I told him that I'd find the guy who'd stolen my bike and beat him up. When he discovered that I didn't know how to fight, he offered to teach me. That's how I got into boxing.[3]

Unlike Muhammed Ali, quoted above, I was never a champion of the ring myself, but I did have adults who reached out to me, too—several of them. And it has made all the difference in my life. I remember Mr. Bidleman, for instance, my junior high Sunday School teacher. He would take a ragtag group of junior highers way upstairs in the choir loft and pour his life into us every week. He would work so hard to make those Sunday School lessons exciting and real, all while keeping a very energetic group of kids focused and on target. As if that weren't enough, he sponsored and attended all the youth functions and helped coach the church basketball team. Then he started a 4-H club in the church and was constantly there guiding us through the ranks of that program.

Talk about availability! Mr. Bidleman's life could be summed

. . . . .

Grandkids in Heaven

My mom died of cancer when I was twenty-three. Her last words were that she would be able to see her grandkids in heaven. At the time I was newly married and had no plans for kids. Four children later, her words still ring in my ears. As I look back, I see that because of her influence and her early death, I've raised my family differently than I would have otherwise. I had become a Christian at eighteen, but really made the commitment when my kids were born.

J.E. Worthington, OH

. . . . .

up in three glorious words: give, give, give.

Fourth, Trumpet the Basic Principles ____

The final step is to be a heritage evangelist. Proclaim the good news of what can happen when adults take those first three steps above. Pull other adults aside and let them know how they can be involved. Here are the basic principles you'll be conveying to them in word and action:

- All young people need a heritage. While it is crucial to pay special attention to those youth who have the least, nearly all children and adolescents need a strong heritage to get them through life.

- Relationships are key. The central conductor for extending a heritage is strong relationships between adults and young people, between young people and their peers, and between teenagers and children.

- Everyone can be a heritage extender. Passing on a heritage requires transmitting consistent messages across a community. All adults, youth, and children play a role.

- Consistent messages need repeating. Extending a heritage requires handing down consistent, positive messages about what is important. Kids need to hear the same positive messages and feel support, over and over again, from many different people.

- It's an ongoing process. Heritage extending starts when a child is born and continues through high school and beyond.

You have the experience, the wisdom, and the heritage to pass. But you might be thinking: "Actually, I don't feel I'm the type. With my position in life, I don't think I'd have anything to offer." Not so! The point is: you are in a perfect position to be a heritage extender.

Who Can Offer an Extended Heritage?

We only need to recall the many family members and friends we've met over the years—heritage extenders, all—to know that you can do it too. Those folks believe the same things about the heritage as we do. They want to give it, and they are shaping children accordingly. The job they're accomplishing is heartening. In addition to parents, some are aunts and uncles, grandparents, single adults, childless couples, teachers . . . the list goes on. So the answer to the question "Who?" is any relative or friend, anyone who knows what a heritage is and wants to extend it into the lives of others. But for now, let's just look at four types of "parenting" that can extend a heritage.

Grandparenting: Your Wisdom Is Needed

How could I ever forget the week-long trip each summer to Pipestone, Minnesota to visit Grandma? I'd usually be with my cousin Jimmy, and then later with my brother Mike. What a treat it was to spend that time with Grandma Koster—listening to the stories she used to tell us into the wee hours of the night, taking the walks "uptown," touring Main Street, going to church with her on Sunday, and, of course, stuffing our faces with her famous peanut butter cookies. Nobody yet has ever made cookies as scrumptious as Grandma's.

God bless grandparents who are just exactly that—grand parents. Some look at that stage of their lives as the time to get away from kids: "I raised mine, now you raise yours." But if the empty nest means we are supposed to abandon the lives of our children and their children and only offer a small, paltry, insignificant amount of time with them, then maybe we should be called grandpittance, rather than grandparents. The Bible, however, has a different view:

A good man leaves an inheritance for his children's children (Prov. 13:22a).

Children's children are a crown to the aged (Prov. 17:6a).

Many grandparents, full of love for their children and their children's children, recognize the great opportunity to teach and inculcate values by passing them on to the third generation. The grand in front of the title parent simply means a parent higher in rank. Parent is a word that means to produce and maintain. Being a grandparent means you've been promoted in rank— given more in title and authority—to maintain what has been produced. And you've earned that right! Writer E.A. Proulx said it like this:

I certainly don't regret becoming a writer later in life because I know a lot more about life than I did twenty years ago, or ten years ago. I think it's important to know how the water's gone over the dam before you start to describe it. It helps to have been over the dam yourself.[4]

Yes, we've seen a lot of water go over the dam in our lives. We've probably rafted a few rapids too. Thus we have great amounts of wisdom to convey to those still sitting on the river-banks. Grandparents, your influence can give a heritage beyond even your immediate family. If you have no grandchildren around, adopt some. Look for couples who are lost and befuddled in their job of parenting, or for children of single parents, or for kids unintentionally abandoned by overworked, overextended parents.

Help guide them through the rough waters. You've been there, done that. Aunts, uncles, cousins—whatever relation you are to children, you can extend and connect and offer solid direction. This is true, even if much of your own learning has come through some painful mistakes. You have learned and grown through those trials, nevertheless. As the great preacher Charles Spurgeon once said: "Train up your child in the way in which you know you should have gone yourself."

Repeat Parenting: Extend Yourself—Again!

A few years ago, I was speaking at a conference with a number of fifty-plus individuals present. After I finished speaking on heritage-building, a stream of people came up to the podium afterward to talk about their lives. I suddenly became aware of another type of parenting that is becoming more and more prevalent in our society today. Called "repeat" parenting, it describes the situation in which grandparents must become the primary caregivers to their grandchildren. Or it could be uncles or aunts becoming the primary caregivers to their nieces and nephews. Usually this situation is triggered by a child born out of wedlock, a broken marriage, financial setbacks, and even substance abuse by the grandparents' adult children.

I talked with many of these couples at great length. My heart went out to them as they explained the great difficulty and challenge in parenting for the second time around. The problem wasn't that they didn't have the time to give; it wasn't because they didn't have the financial resources. No, the point they made was that it's just so different from the "old days."

Parenting the second time around is truly different. Raising today's kids is a radical departure from what it once was. And that fact showed up in the pained faces of these second-timers. It made me want to help them in any way I could.

It also made me think about my own situation. As I look back on my family—my brothers and sisters and my mother— it's apparent to me that, in reality, throughout the last twenty-five years my mother has often found herself in the repeat-parenting role. From time to time, she's had to become the primary caregiver for one of her grandchildren. As I look at those times when she stepped in and became much more involved than what a traditional grandparent would have been, I can only see the wonderful selflessness in her.

Repeat parents are bless-ed. If you are one of them, we're sure you will reap a great blessing too—if not now, then later. But what can the rest of us do to help ease some of the pain when someone enters this repeat parenting role? For one thing, we can encourage them to become involved in parenting classes in their church, while we encourage churches to welcome grandparents who are now in this difficult and challenging role.

We might also encourage other church members to come alongside of repeat parents in order to help relieve some of their pain, their frustrations, their pressure. Suppose repeat parents were invited to spend time with younger parents so they could engage in mutual sharing and learning? Are we willing to bridge the generation gap in such a practical, healing way?

Sidewalk Parenting: Welcome to Your Neighborhood!

Comedian Buddy Hackett once quipped, "My parents were too poor to have children, so the neighbors had me." For many of the kids around us, there is much truth in that statement. Their parents may or may not be poor, but they are often absent, nonetheless. Can we help?

I remember a warm, sunny day when I had just finished mowing the lawn. As I knelt down to clean off my mower, I heard a little voice from out of nowhere: "Whatcha doin'?" (It was too feeble to be the voice of God, so I was more startled than afraid.) As I turned around, I faced a little boy about six years old, kneeling down beside me, taking a look at my cleaning efforts.

"Well, I've just finished mowing the lawn, and now I'm

cleaning up my lawn mower."

"Need any help?"

"Uh, I think I can finish this up by myself."

Next thing I knew, he was gone. Vanished into thin air.

A week went by, and I was into my lawn mowing routine once again, almost at the exact moment of cleaning up my lawn mower when, once again I heard: "Whatcha doin'?" I turned around, and it was the same little neighbor boy. Well, this time I asked him what his name was, and he told me. He again asked me if he could help, and this time I told him, "Sure."

I directed him over to a leaf bag and told him to put some of the grass clippings in it. As he was helping me, we began to talk. I asked him where he lived, and he said he lived a number of blocks away with his mother. Then, quite matter of factly, he stopped and looked at me and said, "But my daddy doesn't live with us anymore."

"Oh, I'm sorry to hear that."

But then he thought for a second and he looked at me with those big eyes and said, "That's okay. My daddy isn't a very nice man."

My heart went out to that little boy. I have wondered since, how many other children are in this neighborhood in the same condition? Maybe the single mother is working fulltime, trying her best to provide. Maybe a relative is repeat parenting but finding too few hours in the day. Maybe the dad—or the mom—just isn't very nice.

That day I tried to become a "sidewalk parent."

A sidewalk parent is a person who befriends and cares about the children in his neighborhood. It's akin to the caring and availability I spoke of earlier, but it goes a step further—by taking steps out the front door.

We realize that this is a very difficult type of parent to become. You see, we're living in a day and age in which sometimes a good-hearted stranger's interest in children is misunderstood. And sadly, some strangers are not good-hearted; we've all heard the stories of abuse. So we must operate with a bit of caution as a sidewalk parent. But one of the greatest things we can do for kids in our neighborhoods is to be out there on the sidewalks with them.

A number of months ago, my wife and I were on a little walk, as we like to do in the evenings. As we wandered a few blocks from our home, we saw a couple of kids playing in a front yard. As is typical, they were ignoring us, and in the past we would have tended to ignore them. But this time, we kind of turned around and said hi and asked what they were doing. They didn't say much, just said they were playing, and as we strolled another twenty yards down the road, one of them stood up and called, "Hey! Did you know there are snakes in the neighborhood?"

We turned around and said, "No, we didn't know there were any snakes around here." He said, "Well, we saw one in our yard today, so you better be careful." We thanked him for his insight and caution and then went our way again.

That was the start of something. Yes, a small start. But how many times do we walk through a mall, and as we come to a group of kids, walk the other way? Suppose we were to just look at them, eye to eye, and say, "Hello. How are you doing today?" Would not that, of its own, communicate value to them?

I don't know what is the right way, the best way to communicate to children today. But we do know that a great number of children are hurting. They don't feel safe in their schools, they may not even feel safe in their homes. But when a loving Christian adult acknowledges their existence, develops a conversation (which may or may not lead to a teachable moment), and shows concern—that is what sidewalk parenting is all about.

Volunteer Parenting: Who, Me? _____

Yes, you. Have you considered getting involved with church and community organizations that help support children?

Getting involved is a fantastic way to make a difference in your community. Most communities have a volunteer center or some other venue where volunteers can help meet local needs. Call that place today. Find out what you can do to make a difference.

Probably the easiest way to become involved with kids is by volunteering in your church. For example, have you ever taught Sunday School? been a vacation Bible school teacher? gotten involved as an advisor in your middle school or teen youth groups? worked in the nursery? These are great opportunities to come alongside of kids, to befriend them, and to make a difference in their lives.

A coworker once shared this story of how a Sunday School teacher made a difference in his life. He said, "I don't remember much of what Mrs. Sorenson taught me in Sunday School over the years. But she had an immeasurable impact on me. After I graduated from her grade school Sunday School class, she kept track of me. She sent a birthday card and encouraging note every year through my teen years. As I went off to college, those cards kept coming. When I got married, she sent a card. When my kids were born, she sent cards. Then she added my kids to her list.

"Through the years, in hard times and good times, Mrs. Sorenson's cards were a reminder that someone out there knew me and cared about me. A few years ago, my mother called with some sad news: Mrs. Sorenson had died. Three days later, my daughter, a college student, received a birthday card—the last one Mrs. Sorenson sent. Mrs. Sorenson sent out two- to three-hundred cards every month to her own list of more than a thousand people she'd met over the years and kept track of. People like me.

"Mrs. Sorenson had a gift. She could see me the way God sees me. She cared, she loved, and she showed her love in her own special way. She was faithful to the gift God had given her and God used that gift to touch me and a lot other people."

As this chapter comes to a close, we want to leave you with

this thought: Remember that volunteering doesn't have to be a formal event or tied to any particular organization. That may be the route you take. But at the most basic level, it is a matter of volunteering of your *self*, no matter where you are. It can be done in countless creative ways. If you're looking for practical ideas to get you started, we'll just list a few we've thought of:

- Spend some extended time in silence—to remember what it was like to be young.
- Learn the names of teenagers in your neighborhood.
- Hug a child or teenager.
- Greet young people with a smile when you pass them on the street.
- Volunteer to be a Big Brother or Sister to a young person through a mentoring program in your community.
- Donate children's and teens' books to a local shelter that serves families and children.
- If you are an employer, hire a teenager to work in your business two afternoons a week—offer plenty of training, support, and encouragement.
- Call a young person you know just to say hi.
- Be a youth advocate—know the issues that affect young people and speak out on their behalf.
- If you're a parent, ask a child to help you with a project; explain what you are doing, why, and how.
- Go to a performance or sporting event of a child or teenager you know.
- Get involved in a youth program within your congregation or community center.
- Hire young people, rather than professionals, to mow your lawn, shovel snow, or rake leaves.

- Go for a walk with a kid.

- Befriend a young person who seems lonely or bored.

Former first lady Barbara Bush once made a truly wonderful statement about the priorities required for extending the heritage. She said: "At the end of your life, you will never regret not having passed one more test, not winning one more verdict, or not closing one more deal. You will regret time not spent with a husband, a friend, a child, or a parent." My friend, you have the experience, the wisdom, and the heritage to pass. Create the time; others need you.

> Chapter 4 <

Being Intentional
about Bridges

⁂

*I*n the state of Colorado, where I (Randy) live, we have
what's billed as the nation's highest suspension bridge. At 1,153
feet above the ground, it spans the Royal Gorge, a magnificent,
rocky gash in the earth that some have likened to a mini Grand
Canyon. What a massive testament to human planning, hard
labor, and sheer perseverance!

As tourists stroll across the wood-planked expanse, they can
look straight down through airy space to the Arkansas River
shimmering like a silver ribbon below. Rafters float by like tiny
play-toys.

A trip to the Royal Gorge reminds every visitor that bridge
building is truly a great art and an exacting science. Hundreds
of miles of twisted steel make up the cables holding the bridge
together, yet the work that started in the 1920s began with a single arrow, shot from one side to the other, attached to a thin
piece of string.

After that simple beginning, it was time for years of follow-
through.

PRINCIPLE: There are relationship chasms in families and community that need to be spanned.

INTENTIONAL IMPACT: I will become a bridge builder.

Start Building Your Bridge

Extending a heritage is, in many ways, like building a strong suspension bridge. It takes dedicated planning, hard work, and a no-looking-back commitment to following through. How many of us have quickly gotten excited by a new ministry opportunity—only to let our passion cool as other concerns pushed their way onto our priority lists? Yet if we truly want to make a difference in others' lives by extending our heritage, we must shoot that first arrow—and then not stop building until all the strong cables are in place, the planking is laid, and travelers are enjoying safe passage.

> . . . . .
>
> ## Godly Grandparents
>
> My grandparents led me to the Lord by their lifestyle. My grandmother always talked about Jesus with so much love and affection, and my grandfather would play gospel records for me to go to sleep with when I stayed at their house. Those things made me want to know this precious Jesus that they so loved.
>
> *B.D. Big Bear Lake, CA*
>
> . . . . .

You see, a bridge connects one land mass to another. Quite often, it arches over a chasm, a canyon, a body of water, or something that separates the two sides. The bridge provides a vehicle or a medium to bring the two closer. In reality, that's what we must do if we are to impact others by extending a heritage to them. We are simply building bridges of spiritual and cultural transmission. If we are to follow through with our grand plans, we must begin by asking ourselves three critical questions about the bridges we intend to build:

With Whom Do We Build? _____

That is our choice. If we decide we want to extend our heritage to our grandkids, we'll focus on them. Or is it a niece, a nephew, a neighbor kid? The bottom line is that it's up to us. But we will not move forward if we don't first clearly identify whom we're trying to reach. We know it's something that we must have on our mind at all times. If we want to impact children for Christ within our neighborhood, for instance, we must be available and we must be sensitive to their existence.

All of this usually requires going out of our way. Suppose we want to extend our heritage to a niece or nephew living out of state. It won't happen unless we are intentional and inconvenienced. In other words, we must identify areas of mutual interest, plan for times when we can connect, and then make all the necessary arrangements to maintain contact.

Another thing to remember: not only do we need to build bridges with the child, but also with the child's parents. Certainly, we can't ignore the parents; that benefits no one. The parents have been given the primary responsibility for conveying their heritage. It is our purpose simply to come alongside of the parents in such a way as to support and complement what they are doing. Now in the cases where the heritage being passed is not complete, either from a social, emotional, or spiritual perspective, we can then help to fill in the void. But this only works with the blessing of the parents.

"Wait a minute," you might say. "My children have fallen away from the Lord and are almost anti-God. They aren't raising my grandchildren in the love and admonition of the Lord, and it breaks my heart. What can I do about it?" In those cases, again, we need to discuss the situation with the parents. If there is such deep animosity evident (though very rarely does it reach this point, because even non-believers seem to know that the Bible and Sunday School are good starting points for their children), there's not much you can do until the parents come around. Offering a heritage is just that: an offer. It can't become a subtle exercise in manipulation, and it should never be forced over a parent's wishes.

We can only be there, ready to offer support. And we can rely on the leading of the Holy Spirit to identify opportunities to come alongside and start opening the door for those children to develop a relationship with Jesus Christ. The reality is that in most cases, parents will encourage you as long as you're not doing something in direct opposition to them.

What Size Do We Make It?

Not only do we need to build a bridge, we've got to determine its best size. We're talking about the amount of time and energy dedicated to any particular relationship. Of course, that depends a lot on the one being mentored and on the circumstances involved. This is a growing relationship, and as the relationship grows, the opportunities to extend our heritage increase dramatically.

A number of years ago, I started a men's group. We met once a week on Monday evenings in my home. I remember how frustrating the first year was, as it was so difficult to get down to meaningful, open discussions that went deeper than the latest football scores. We met for almost six years, though it probably wasn't until year two that we finally moved to a level of intimacy that I had longed for. It took that long to build bridges among the guys in that group and to find common ground for sharing. Some assumptions had to be overcome; barriers had to come down. Quite often, these barriers are self-created, determined by false perceptions of others' motives or roles.

Similar things occur when we adults attempt to work with

children. Children tend to view parents, or any adults, as authority figures whose primary purpose is to tell them what to do. Adults are rarely viewed by children as persons to go to for encouragement, reinforcement, or friendship. And sadly, we, as adults, usually enter into a relationship with a child from a standpoint of superiority. We have the knowledge and experience, and thus we may direct the construction of this bridge with a heavy-handed leadership.

Yet we can be learners, too. After all, Jesus once said: "I tell you the truth, anyone who will not receive the kingdom of God like a little child will never enter it" (Luke 18:17). Maybe we should stop and rethink our role with kids. They seem pretty important!

The point is, the size of the bridge is determined by the level of our transparency.

. . . . .

Preaching Kids

My father was a preacher, and he would have us give some of his written sermons on family nights. We would use a TV tray as a pulpit and then deliver the message in our best preacher voice. I am now a full-time minister.

R.J. Frisco, TX

. . . . .

Open yourself up a little. Be vulnerable. We know it's difficult, but relationships grow and thrive only as human beings choose—dare!—to reveal their true selves. You are not perfect, and children need not believe you are. All you require is to be respected; you will give respect in return.

Friend, we're just inviting you to be real in your efforts. Don't put on airs, don't try to make yourself into something you're not. As you are true to who you are, that essential integrity will be much more effective than any exciting facade you could create. Children can see right through phoniness, anyway. They know how to go to the heart of an issue, and they know how to go to the heart of a person. Transparency and vulnerability greatly increase the size of our bridge. They bring height, depth, and width to any relationship.

How Far Do We Go?

When have we gone far enough? When have we gone too far? When is the process complete? With a literal bridge, the answers are obvious. In a heritage-extending relationship, the answers come only with wise discernment, in time. Often, circumstances alone will answer the questions. Perhaps the child moves out of town. Maybe he or she finds some other adult who can meet a different set of needs or speak to a different set of concerns. As a child grows, things change, times change, needs change. Kids move into different circles of influence. They reach a new level of maturity, they grow up. In other situations, the relationship will continue to grow, right on through adulthood.

We do go through various stages of our lives with children. In the beginning, we are the protector, the provider of safety and security. Later on, we become the depositor of knowledge, the teacher. A little later on, we move into more of a coaching role, content to stand on the sidelines, encouraging, providing support as needed, cheering them on to success. In this final stage, it is now their skills that matter the most; they are on the field and making the big decisions.

We might say that the final stage for us is to play the role of consultant. Once children have grown up and moved on, we are still the keeper of knowledge, experience, and maturity. But we are mainly available "by request," when that grown child has a particular need, opens the door, and invites us to enter into mutual problem-solving.

Clearly, we must be sensitive to the natural growth in the relationship, always ready to grow and to modify our style of helping. In reality, all children need heritage builders throughout their lives. It is so important for us to come alongside, at all stages, to convey what our experience has taught us.

Make It a Two-Lane Passage! _____

When it comes to heritage extending, we'll want a double-lane bridge that allows for traffic going in both directions. This is a key characteristic to extending a heritage. A single-lane, one-way bridge takes a person from point A to point B, but never allows for the return trip, never allows for the return feedback, and only focuses on the destination. Throughout our task of building relationships, it's crucial that we create two-way communication. Observing a few relational rules will help.

Observe the Seven Rules of Mentoring _____

Certain characteristics of heritage extending are typically part of a meaningful and successful experience. Let us identify what we consider these key characteristics. You may have some of your own to add, but we've summed them up in seven statements that help us the most.

1. Offer respect, build trust. Respect and trust always seem to go together. How can we communicate respect to a child? For one thing, we become good listeners. We ask questions and care about how kids respond. We acknowledge them when we meet them on a walk or at a store. We make them feel important.

This is something I've had to learn the hard way. I've always been a task-oriented and driven person. I make up my mind that I want to do something, and I do it. In my desire to reach my goals, though, I tend to push and drive to conclusion rather than enjoying the journey. I'm not likely to stop and smell the roses. Are you that way, too? If so, slow down! Allow situations to develop and evolve. A child picks up on our drivenness immediately, and usually pulls back and shuts down; a barrier begins to evolve between us.

It's sad, but very few children today seem to trust adults, and our drivenness may be a big reason. Kids have been lied to, ignored, taken advantage of, and in some cases abused, emotionally and physically. In light of these things, much of the media teaches children not to trust adults. Kids are told that adults cannot understand or relate to them. However, if we approach this problem wisely, we can earn their trust by showing ourselves consistently trustworthy. When kids share, we'll treat their words seriously and maintain confidentiality. Another way to earn trust is simply to be there when we say we will be there. When you say you are going to do something, do it. Enough said?

2. Identify common ground. What is the leveler within a relationship? It's the common area of contact. Is it sports? love of rock music? the joy of fishing? an interest in chess? the thrill of frog catching?

What particular activities are helping you and your new friend establish a common vocabulary, a common relationship, and a common perception to build on? In the identification of common ground we can evaluate a child's need. With the neighborhood child who worked with me on the lawn, it became apparent to me,

.....

Body of Christ

When we moved into our house, we were newly married with no kids. Since moving in we've endured cancer, the death of my mom, three kids, new jobs, and depression, but we were not alone. God placed us right between three other young, Christian couples with kids. It is so helpful raising our kids with families of similar values and struggles. It truly exemplifies the body of Christ.

T.R., Carrollton, TX

.....

while we bagged grass, that he needed an adult male who cared about him. As our relationship developed, he began to get what he needed—and I had more energy left after my dreaded weekly chores.

Identifying common ground means majoring in shared experience, even if it's just yard work. Or go to ball games together, to concerts, or just go to the store. Create common experiences. And one other thing in this regard: as you have opportunity, give practical help, not just theory. Children live in the here and now. That's why the activity you're doing together isn't just a side issue. It's what's happening, now. Kids have difficulty in relating to theory or abstract concepts. They tend to be do-it-now or solve-it-now people. It's important that we stay focused and practical with anything we share or do to help.

3. Model appropriate behavior. Children don't miss a thing. We're sure you've discovered this. They observe and internalize, cutting right through the phoniness. They're quick to pick up on inconsistencies between what they are being told and what they are seeing. That's why doing an activity with a kid is more important than trying to devise a teaching session, as author/businessman Patrick Morley discovered:

> *My son wanted to help change a flat tire on my car. He couldn't loosen the lug nuts. He ran out of energy to unscrew them all. He couldn't lift the old tire off or put the new one on. Once the new tire was on, he tried to get away with only putting on every other lug nut. It took twice as long with his help.*
>
> *While he couldn't help me as much as he thought he could, he went away thinking he had helped me more than he did. The experience made a large spiritual impression on him. His self-esteem grew by a mile, and now he understands the concepts of diligence and excellence in a deeper way. Those are biblical values, and I impressed them upon my son in a way that was natural, not contrived. I wasn't teaching him how to change a flat tire; I was teaching him how to be a man of God.[1]*

The best way to influence children is to be a great role model, to live out your faith in everything you do. The Apostle

Paul said: "Whatever you have learned or received or heard from me, or seen in me—put it into practice" (Phil. 4:9a). That is the way we, too, can approach our young mentorees. When we fail—and we will fail—we need not be afraid. Admit it, ask for forgiveness, and move on.

4. *Accept different styles.* Learning styles vary among human beings. Have you noticed? Some children learn best visually, by what they observe. Some learn best through what they hear. Others are much more hands-on, tactile, and learn best by doing. We, of course, must learn to adapt to our young friend's best method of learning. Actually, younger children learn in all three ways, because they haven't developed a primary preference yet. So we must adjust our style as we observe their responses. The key point, though, is to avoid squelching a child's natural curiosity and zest for life.

> *A little boy sees and hears birds with delight. Then the "good father" comes along and feels he should "share" the experience and help his son "develop." He says: "That's a jay, and this is a sparrow." The moment the little boy is concerned with which is a jay and which is a sparrow, he can no longer see the birds or hear them sing. He has to see and hear them the way his father wants him to.*
>
> *Father has good reasons on his side, since few people can afford to go through life listening to the birds sing, and the sooner the little boy starts his "education" the better. . . . A few people, however, can still see and hear in the old way. But most of the members of the human race have lost the capacity . . . and are not left the option of seeing and hearing directly, even if they can afford to; they must get it second-hand.[2]*

Some of us had parents who told us: "My way or the highway." If we didn't do a task just the way Daddy did it, then it wasn't good enough. How sad! Be sure to let the youngster you're mentoring have free reign in interpreting the experiences that come her way. You'll be able to gently correct and guide later, if need be. But in the moment, go with the flow.

5. *Seize the teachable moments.* One of the greatest things we've learned as a heritage extenders is to be sensitive to the leading of the Holy Spirit in identifying teachable moments. A dear friend of ours, and a true heritage builder, shared an experience he had with his family. They had enjoyed a Family Night, having discussed the power of prayer in daily life. The next day, the kids hopped into the car and headed off with their father for a trip to the hardware store. When they got home, Dad found he no longer had his checkbook with him.

He headed back to the store to see where he had lost it, but it was nowhere to be found. Frustration, dejection, and disappointment set in. But as he got back into the car, one of his children said, "Dad, maybe we should just stop and pray about it. Just like you taught us last night."

Well, Dad thought that was a unique approach—something he wished he'd thought of first! He and the kids sat right there in the store's parking lot and prayed for the return of a checkbook. Several days later, a package arrived in the mail. When opened, out popped Dad's checkbook. What a confirmation of the power of prayer, and what encouragement to the children! Was this a teachable moment? Definitely. Even though it was initiated by the kids. (Quite often, that is how those moments arise.)

6. *Listen aggressively, communicate effectively.* Again we have two items that always go together: listening and speaking. High up on the list of children's frustrations with adults is the fact that adults just don't seem to listen. Years ago, as the owner of a small business that created and sold Christian toys and gifts, I marketed a game called Kids' Choices. Each player would receive a Moral Dilemma Card and a Scripture Card. On the dilemma card was an actual moral dilemma that a child might face in life. On the

Scripture card were five verses that would speak to that moral dilemma in some way. It was the responsibility of each person in the game to read his moral dilemma aloud, state how he would respond, and then identify one of the Scripture texts that supported his response.

We received dozens of letters over the years from parents who were so impressed with how their children responded to the moral dilemmas—with what intelligence and maturity they responded. Our question is, did the game itself bring out this wisdom from the child? Or was the wisdom always there, and because of the game's format, it forced adults to listen a little more closely to their child's thought processes?

7. *Pull out the stops—with affirmation.* What do we mean by pulling out the stops? It's an expression related to playing the pipe organ. When the organist wants to fill an auditorium with vast reverberations of sound, she pulls out all the knobs on that organ so the wind can flow at full force through the sound pipes.

You want to fill the child with esteem and a deep-down, rumbling sense of worth? Well . . . pull out the stops and let her have it! Let your affirmations wash over kids, day in and day out. It's true that self-esteem comes from proving oneself accountable and responsible—not just from being praised. Yet when kids do come through and accomplish significant things, no matter how small—let them hear the sweet music of your commendation.

Affirm any growth, any successes that children experience as you work with them in extending your heritage. Children get so little affirmation today. They are continually being told what they do wrong, rarely told what they do right. We, as adults, are highly critical and communicate continual dissatisfaction. Just the other day, I was sitting out on my deck observing a beautiful Saturday morning. Our neighbor was cutting some weeds next to his house. This man is probably in his late fifties, and his son was visiting from out of town, a young man in his midtwenties.

Oh, how my wife and I sat there and chuckled as we listened to the father continually directing his son, telling him to watch out for that flower and this rock, and to make sure that he changed from shorts to long pants so he wouldn't hurt himself. The poor guy wasn't doing this right, and he was doing that all wrong.

We chuckled, but it was, at heart, a truly sad sight. Yet any of us parents—grand, volunteer, repeat, or sidewalk—can fall into that negative approach to parenting. Perhaps we're too afraid of children growing up, and leaving, and never coming back. But then, what things are we doing to push them away?

Expect Nothing in Return _____

Extending a heritage is a thoroughly rewarding experience. And we firmly believe that as you launch out in bridge building, your rewards will be great. But that is not why you do it. That cannot be your primary motivation.

We adults are so bottom-line oriented that if there isn't a quick return, or the return doesn't appear large enough, we begin to question the value of what we're putting into the cause. Yet the ultimate goal of heritage extending is the opposite of selfishness. In fact, our task is to work ourselves out of a job. We are looking for people to take our place in society. Just as Moses trained Joshua to take his place, just as Jesus trained His disciples to be "little Christs" in the

. . . . .

Pay Your Debts

My dad taught me to always pay your debts and bills. Once when my dad owed a man for some work, he drove across town and walked out to a field where a man was plowing with his tractor to pay him for his service. That incident has always stuck with me as to how important it is to pay others, whatever it takes to do that.

D.S. Sterling, CO

. . . . .

world, so we are training young people to be what we have
been. The reward is in the self-relinquishment—which is the
essence of spiritual growth.

If children think we're doing this for the wrong motivations
and that we are more interested in our own glory than in them
as human beings, they will end up declining our offers of guid-
ance. It is important that we just focus on the child and not the
end results.

Yet let us remember that we are, indeed, making end results
every day, with everyone we meet. We think the great defender
of Christianity, C.S. Lewis, summed this idea up so well that
we'll leave you with his words:

> It is a serious thing to live in a society of possible gods and
> goddesses, to remember that the dullest and most uninterest-
> ing person you can talk to may one day be a creature which, if
> you saw it now, you would be strongly tempted to worship, or
> else a horror and a corruption such as you now meet, if at all,
> only in a nightmare. All day long we are, in some degree,
> helping each other to one or other of these destinations. . . .
> There are no ordinary people. You have never talked to a mere
> mortal.[3]

⁂ *Chapter 5* ⁂

Using All the Tools to Extend Your Heritage

*M*en are famous for never using them although they practically come with every product that requires any assembly at all. I (J. Otis) put my children's bikes together without them. I assembled trains, model planes, light fixtures, lawn equipment, and you name it and never used them. Now, I'm not saying I never had parts left over—that's none of anybody's business— but everything worked nonetheless. Even when my old 1956 Ford blew a head gasket, my college roommate and I replaced it without them. Yes, we had parts left over, didn't we Sonny McCaskill? But the car worked and you are my witness that we drove it home, 360 miles away.

Of course I am speaking of instructions. Notwithstanding my abuse of them, they are an important part of life. I think, as I grow older, I understand better their function. Anyway, I use them more now than before. So I feel perfectly okay with what I am about to suggest. When passing a heritage, use the instructions and have proper tools!

If there are no ordinary people, and if we have never talked to a mere mortal as C. S. Lewis suggested, then it becomes very important for us to be familiar with some available tools to accomplish the extending of our heritage. It also becomes vital that we know how to use those tools.

> **PRINCIPLE**: To extend our heritage, tools and resources are needed to accomplish the task.

> **INTENTIONAL IMPACT**: To help the heritage extender to be confident and accomplished in the use of the various Heritage Builders tools.

The Heritage Chart _____

The use of the tools in an extending parenting role will differ from the use of the immediate family role. But the process still follows the same path.

Take a look at the way the chart on the next page flows. It begins with the heritage, and wends its way through to the tools. The flow is important to the sustained effort of heritage extending. A firm understanding of the framework leads to a firm grasp of the use of the tools.

Instructions _____

The instructions are simple. The extending of your heritage is the goal. If you're a couple, husband and wife must evaluate what type of spiritual, emotional, and social legacies they individually bring into the relationship. As most couples find, both will bring a mixed bag of each legacy. For example, the wife will bring both strong and weak elements of her spiritual legacy as will the husband. It is here where hard work must be done. Sometimes it isn't easy to evaluate your past. Guilt along with other barriers will block your efforts, but keep moving forward.

If you are a single adult, then a thorough evaluation of your

The Heritage Builders Concept

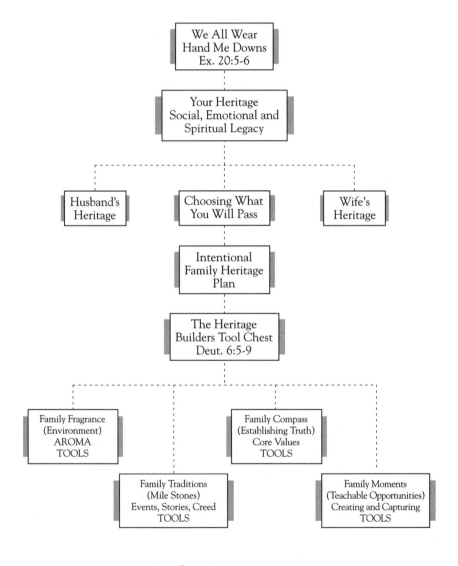

We All Wear
Hand Me Downs
Ex. 20:5-6

Your Heritage
Social, Emotional and
Spiritual Legacy

Husband's
Heritage

Choosing What
You Will Pass

Wife's
Heritage

Intentional
Family Heritage
Plan

The Heritage
Builders Tool Chest
Deut. 6:5-9

Family Fragrance
(Environment)
AROMA
TOOLS

Family Compass
(Establishing Truth)
Core Values
TOOLS

Family Traditions
(Mile Stones)
Events, Stories, Creed
TOOLS

Family Moments
(Teachable Opportunities)
Creating and Capturing
TOOLS

Psalm 78: 1 - 8

heritage is also needed. There will be no integration process since your legacies are the only ones being considered, but choices need to be made as to what you intend to keep and what you plan to replace.

Please understand, we are not asking you to judge the job your parents did in raising you and your siblings. We are asking you to evaluate how you perceived what they were trying to accomplish. Four siblings can be raised in the same household with the same rules, and each perceives them differently. Each person's perception usually determines his or her personal response. That response can be as different as light and dark. So evaluate your perceptions, not your parents' intentions. Your perception of the heritage you were given will be critical to the one you will extend to others. A clear understanding will result in a clearer plan as you pick those people you will extend toward.

Use the evaluation forms beginning on page 133 to review the strengths and weaknesses in your heritage.

Choices

Now, decisions at this juncture are critical. With the evaluations in front of you, as a couple or as a single adult, make the decisions as to what will be kept from your legacies, and what will be tossed. There may be parts of each legacy that are good but weak. A decision may be made here to keep the weak components, but form a plan to strengthen them.

For instance, you may find the "enforcement of rules" part of your social legacy was weak. Perhaps rules were more important

> *• • • • •*
>
> ### *Prayer Circle*
>
> My neighbor had her children stand in a circle and one sibling would pray for another before school. What a great way to teach intercessory prayer.
>
> *K.R. Sanford, NC*
>
> *• • • • •*

than relationships. The entire plan for rules does not need to be discarded, just strengthened. Like I say, one doesn't burn down the house to get rid of the roaches! So, lay out your plan to blend the rules of your home with relationships.

Integration of the Legacies

In a Heritage Builders workshop in Ventura, California a curious thing happened. We had spent the morning explaining the heritage passing process. We gave instructions and inspiration, then asked the participants to fill out the evaluation forms. That is always an interesting time because eyes become wide at the conclusion of this session. Some—for the first time—are face to face with their legacies.

One brave mom and dad took the lunch hour and left to have lunch with their children. They have a teen daughter and son. Mom and Dad asked their children to take the evaluation, giving them permission to be brutally honest. The result was fascinating. Dad's score was high on each of the legacies, but his wife's score was weak. She came from an abusive homelife. While sitting at lunch, they discovered that their children's scores were the average of Mom and Dad's scores combined. On the emotional legacy, Mom scored an eight and Dad scored a twenty-eight. Both children scored an eighteen. The children were receiving a copy of Mom and Dad's mixed bag.

After your evaluations and choices comes the integration. The choices that come from your individual heritage should be on paper in front of you. Now list the components of each legacy you plan to keep. List each you plan to strengthen, then if you're doing this as a couple begin, as it were, to superimpose them on top of each other. Where one is missing components the other will fill the void. Take your time. This process is critical. You are making decisions as to how your household will function. How will you balance rules and relationships? How will you communicate love, words, respect, or spiritual elements like prayer and values? Remember you are merging into a whole the best and leaving behind the bad.

Understanding the Windows of Opportunity

When extending your heritage beyond your family, remember that there are different levels of receptivity to the values you are passing. Children at an early age perceive your involvement in their lives differently than older ones. Study the windows of opportunity chart below. It will help you understand at what age the level of receptivity is at its highest with the child or teen you have chosen to extend toward.

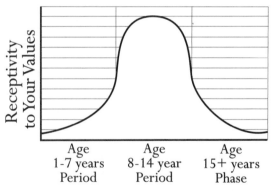

Imprint Impression Coaching

From birth to approximately age seven, children are in the imprint period of life. The level of receptivity to your values is low. They do not yet know how to reason. If you tell them a cat is a dog, they will believe you just because you are grandma or uncle. You can teach them blue is yellow. It will stick with them until they go to school and find out you lied. Then they will wonder why you told them that.

From age seven to approximately age fifteen they are in the

impression period. You will notice that their level of receptivity peaks during this stage. That knowledge is critical because it is a stage that is difficult at best to recapture. At around the age of nine, ten, and eleven they are at the highest level. At about the age of twelve a decline of that receptivity is noticeable. That is because you are nearing the coaching period of their lives—as they are nearing the game phase. That is where they will test the values they have learned against real life situations. If your values don't work, they will find another coach—their peers, a gang, a teacher . . . someone.

It would be wise to memorize this chart, or at least keep it on your refrigerator door, to remind you where you are in the stages of the person's life to whom you are attempting to extend your heritage.

Tools for the Task

Now you are ready to begin the process of extending to others what you were given. This is the most fun and exciting part of all. Stand back, dust off your hands, take a deep breath, and get ready to enjoy. Prepare to delight in the fruit of your labor.

The process for passing your heritage to a person beyond your immediate family is closely related to leaving a legacy to your children. The tools are the same. You will have to improvise their use by altering the way they are implemented. For instance, when helping a child outside your home to set borders, the accountability factor alters, so respect within that relationship becomes preeminent. The correction and punishment factor severely decreases if not completely disappears, so the respect factor will need to sharply increase to experience success.

Let's dig into the tool chest and begin to learn how to use the tools to successfully extend your heritage beyond immediate family.

Family Fragrance

Five key characteristics to a healthy family fragrance contribute to an environment of love in the home. The first is demonstrative love; the second is building esteem with acts of respect. Third is creating a clear structure so everyone and everything has a place. Fourth is the ability to have fun and laugh together as a family. Last is the capstone of an upward spiral the first four create. It is affirmation—building people up instead of tearing them down. All together they are represented by the acrostic AROMA.

A	Affection
R	Respect
O	Order
M	Merriment
A	Affirmation

. . . . .

Hats, Hats, Hats

I was praying for my children to be blessed when a woman we know found out my daughter collects hats. Whenever she finds a hat she thinks my daughter would like, she brings it to her. My daughter has witnessed God's love through a person who barely knew her. Now they are great friends.

N.P., San Benito, TX

. . . . .

Let's take a look at each component in the light of extending your heritage and examine how it may differ from the original in implementation.

Affection: Affection is the outward manifestation of an inward love. It is a powerful tool and one that is eternal. It is interesting to note that of the three important components that exist in this world called faith, hope, and love, the only one that is forever is love. One day we will realize our hope in heaven and hope will no longer be a necessity. Faith will also be an obsolete item in eternity. We will be seeing and

experiencing the object of our faith. But love! It is a forever com-
modity. It, perhaps more than all the rest, shows God in our
lives because He is Love.

Used in the extending the heritage position, this tool must
not be confused with the human contrivance called lust. When
one gender is showing affection to a person of the opposite gender outside family ties, extreme care must be taken. The situation can be shaky ground. Even though touch is important,
other means of showing affection can be practiced.

• Words: Affection can be transmitted by many means.
Words can carry a barrel full of love. Using this tool to build
rather than demolish isn't an art or a science but a discipline. Art
usually takes some level of talent; science takes proving. To use
words takes neither, just a set of eyes to see others as God sees,
then telling someone how you care. It takes a person with a genuine heart for others who can see the good in them when others
can only see the possible bad.

A grandparent may speak words from a distance. Send a
card, alternate the serious with humorous.

Learn to use the internet. Instant messages are very inexpen-
sive. There you can help solve math problems and help them
find research for English projects.

Make appointments for phone calls.

Write letters on special occasions like graduations and
accomplishments in athletics or the arts.

If you are in the same city, a trip to a fast food establishment
to down a Coke and share that day's experiences will open
more lines of communication.

• Touch: Perhaps it has been over quoted, but indulge us
one more time as we quote Smalley and Trent from their book
The Blessing.

In a study at UCLA, it was found that just to maintain emo-
tional and physical health, men and women need eight to ten

meaningful touches each day! These researchers defined mean-
ingful touch as a gentle touch, stroke, kiss, or hug given by
significant people in our lives (a husband or wife, parent,
close friend, and so on). This study estimated that if some
"type A driven" men would hug their wives several times
each day, it would increase their life span by almost two
years! (Not to mention the way it would improve their mar-
riages.) Obviously, we can physically bless those around us
(and even ourselves) with meaningful touch.[1]

Putting this in context with the extended heritage, several cautions need to be voiced. First, be aware of the times in which we live. There are those who have evil intent in their heart and this tool could provide an avenue for distortion. I believe everyone needs hugs. Give them out freely and gladly, but give them with discretion. For instance, if I am extending my heritage to a worthy older, teenaged girl, she does need touch, but she wouldn't receive it in the same manner as my daughter. My sixteen year old sits with me on the couch, lays her head on my shoulder and chest. Sometimes she gets her pillow and curls up with her head and shoulders on my lap. Perfectly normal for her, but perfectly abnormal for someone outside her station.

Find ways to give proper touches. Nothing really substitutes for physical touch, but a card, handwritten notes, homemade goodies, candy, phone call, or flowers well placed in their lives on special days can come close to a touch.

When the person to whom you are extending your heritage is the same gender and a relative, hugs and touch are a wonderful expression—within the bounds of common sense.

Respect: Extending your heritage to another with this component called respect is vital to them. I believe this because I think respectful behavior comes out of a heart that has come to grips with life's ups and downs. I try to help those to whom I extend my heritage to see their situations, however difficult they may be, as what God has given them to solve. It helps them respect their lives so much more.

That test your grandson failed doesn't signal the end of the world. Meet him at the coffee shop at a bookstore or library and help find the answers to the questions he missed, or help read books and find sources for a term paper he may be writing.

Not making the team, whether in sports or dance isn't the end all. Show the teen in your Sunday School class other teams she can be a part of, like the worship team at church, or a team that serves food at the local mission.

How can we work harder? What can be done to change the circumstance?

I try to talk them through the situation so they can take ownership of those circumstances and get involved in the solution instead of being colleagues with the problems.

Everyone deserves respect. It is a two-way street. When you give it, you are likely to get it. Enter each extended relationship with it, and sustain that relationship with it.

Order: There is a time to be born and a time to die. There is a time for everything that occurs between the two. Everybody and everything has a place in life. Extending this part of your heritage to someone floundering in life will help him or her

> • • • • •
> ## A Loving Auntie
>
> While Auntie never came right out and shared her faith with me, I always knew where she stood spiritually. She prayed for me regularly. She loved me and never criticized me through some pretty unlovable stages of my life. As an adult, when I started my walk with Christ, she loaned materials to me that helped me grow. I'm certain that Auntie's prayers covered me with protection during my years of wandering. Auntie is in heaven now, but I will always be thankful for her prayers and God's amazing grace!
>
> *S.W., Mahomet, IL*
>
> • • • • •

bring order to his or her world. Any living thing without order is usually sick. Any inanimate thing without order is usually broke and in need of repair.

James, who has chosen Mike to extend his heritage to, takes him for a ride in his car. Mike is close to the age when he will be getting his driver's license, and James is helping him understand the reasons for traffic laws. All those laws serve to keep cars from colliding and hurting people. By doing what Mike really likes to do, James is able to teach the importance of observing the order of the road. He can apply that lesson to other circumstances of living.

Use this portion of the tool to help stabilize the person you are extending your heritage to if you discover his world is out of kilter. Healthy study habits don't come easy for some children or teens. Setting priorities, even for adults, is a difficult task, let alone for a young person.

The demeanor of her children confuses my secretary when the kids visit her parents without her or her husband around. She has two strong-willed boys who love to compete against each other. It causes some chaos in the home, at times, but at Grandy and Mimi's house the boys are almost angels.

"Why?" Sherry queries.

She and her husband concluded that the boys are competing for who can impress their grandparents with the best behavior. Being savvy grandparents, Mimi and Grandy take that opportunity to concentrate on behavior patterns, helping to teach order in a different yet acceptable setting to the children.

Merriment: Teach them to not take life too seriously. Teach them that laughter does good like a medicine. Show them how to find pleasure in all life's ups and downs. Help them to lighten up, be happy, and understand that worry is a killer.

Life, by its very definition, was given to us to live! So, lighten up!

I love to have fun. I let the people in my congregation know that frequently. Those that Gail and I have chosen to extend our heritage to also know that.

A family that has Sunday dinner with us often is the Krigbaums. Their two little boys call me Uncle Otis. But they are quick to tell people that I am only their fake uncle. "He's not really real," they say.

We have a blast together. They ride home from church with me every week. They especially love it when we are in my classic Datsun 240Z. They call it "Uncle Otis' speed car." The younger boy, Tyler, who is five, likes to tease when he has the best of the situation, but he gets intense when he feels he is losing. We always make up names for those family members who get home before us, or even after us. We call them losers; holding our thumb and index finger in the shape of an L, we point toward them and pronounce them "loooooooooosssssssers."

My son, Matthew, who loves to have fun with the boys, will then banter with them. One day when Tyler thought he was ahead of the "talk" game, Matthew decided to have some fun. He told Tyler, "I may be a loser, but you're king of the hill." Tyler, thinking that must be a derogatory term, said, "Uhn Uh!" loudly with passion and retorted, "You're king of the hill." Now every Sunday, who ever is last to get to the house is pronounced with that "neener-neener" tone of his, "You're king of the hill." We are all looking forward to the day Tyler finds out the true meaning of that phrase.

Even with the teens in our youth department or at our Christian school I love to have a good time. Gail and I try to attend most home sporting events. Often, we are the loudest, especially with Gail's cowbell. It has taken on a legendary quality. All the players want her to clang that bell for them. It annoys some parents and most umps, but sure is fun for us and the teens.

Having good, clean fun is easy. Nothing elaborate is necessary. Be creative. Merriment is infectious.

A single adult can be the source of fun for a child from a home that is tense. Pick her up and play table games at your house with friends. Take him hunting or fishing. Go to a play at a local high school or college.

Long-distance grandparents can bring merriment to their grandchildren by sending gift certificates for ice-cream parlors or create riddles to be solved with rewards for efforts.

One long-distance grandmother told me that she and her husband purchase two puzzles and mix the pieces of both puzzles in one box (easy to medium puzzles). They send a picture of the puzzles and promise a special outing when they visit if the puzzles are solved. If not, it gives them an activity to do together once they are with their grandchildren.

Affirmation: When I am speaking at workshops or retreats, I tell the audience that this part of the tool just happens when the four previous components are attended to. The whole AROMA thing is like an upward spiral, like the aroma ascending from a freshly baked pie. So this tool lifts and lifts by its implementation. It rushes to reach up to affirm. That is indeed aroma's capstone!

Words and actions are the vehicles that transport our affirmation to each individual. So a hug, a pat on the back, or tousling the hair carries with it an unspoken word of declaration. It helps affirm that circumstances are only temporary, and encourages a forward and upward movement that says, "Don't give up or give in." A person who is affirmed by those he or she respects will be an adult who can take on the world.[2]

Family Compass

The family compass is that need to measure every action, attitude, and belief against some objective measure of truth. A compass points to true north. Once that direction has been established, a person can then negotiate his or her way to their destination with confidence. We believe that the only true compass is found in the words of the Holy Scriptures.

One major problem for the family in this culture is the lack of an objective standard. Because of that, moral absolutes are scoffed at, and it becomes easier to get lost in the confusion. Kids are confused about lifestyles, religion, marriage, money, education, and most everything else that requires a standard of measurement.

The circumstances surrounding the tragic death of J.F.K., Jr., and his passengers off Martha's Vineyard in July, 1999 served to remind us of the importance of a compass. When the plane left the ground the conditions were clear, but somewhere in the course of the trip a haze set in and confused all sense of direction. At that point, apparently the human instinct for survival set in and the all-important gauges were abandoned. Kennedy couldn't tell if his wings were parallel with the horizon, and he was unfamiliar with instrument flying rules. The importance of his compass was negated, and tragedy waited only a few minutes away.

Living in a world that is covered with the smog of a postmodern culture does much the same spiritually as the haze did physically. Many lose their bearings. Even though the horizon is blurred, vertical wisdom is abandoned for horizontal living. It doesn't work. They panic! They are not familiar with the territory nor the instruments that will point them to a true and safe destination. They become lost in the smog. A different kind of tragedy awaits them, yet it is a tragedy of greater proportions. It has eternal implications. Can the importance of the family compass be overstated?

It was interesting and encouraging to see what direction the conversation headed after the tragic shootings at some of our public schools. True north was needed. True north was pointed out. Prayer and scriptural values surfaced almost without adversity.

This tool can be used without customization. In extending it to anyone, truth remains the same for all. Help the person to establish some checkpoints along in their daily lives such as self-worth, delayed gratification, personal responsibility, spiritual exploration, and priorities. Help them stop long enough in the haze of all the philosophies to check the compass and adjust everything according to true north.

I was giving a talk in a chapel service at a school about having a family compass to measure all decisions by, when a young man who is a high school junior raised his hand to interrupt.

"What do you mean, compass, and where can we get one?" he asked.

There was the usual chuckle from the other students. But there was no disrespectful tone in his voice, so I asked him if I could answer that question after chapel. I wanted to see if he was serious or being comical.

He stayed afterward!

Before he could ask another question, I started answering the one he asked in assembly. "When you want to find where you came from, check your compass. When you want to know what to wear, check your compass. When you want to know when sexual activity is okay, check the compass. When you want to know what kind of music to listen to and what your relationship should be with your parents and friends—" Before I could finish he interrupted by raising the palm of his hand toward me as if to quiet me and said, "Check my compass."

"Think about it, Tim," I continued. "True north isn't so much a direction as it is a solution. True north excludes all other directional options."

He looked puzzled so I kept going.

"Where did you come from? True north: 'In the beginning God . . .' What should I wear? True north: 'Adorn yourself in modest apparel . . .' What about sex and pornography? True north: 'Flee youthful lust . . .'"

By this time Tim was understanding. He even finished a few of his own questions.

Later I learned that Tim was the son of a single mom. He had no male role model, and his mother worked hard to make it financially. Her job kept her from attending church. I introduced Tim to a man in our church who now is extending his legacy to him. I saw Tim the other day between classes at school, he held up his New Testament and said, "True north."[3]

Family Traditions

Traditions are the bearings on which a heritage glides from generation to generation. They are perhaps some of the most overlooked tools, yet some of the most effective. Ask yourself, "How many traditions does our family observe each year?"

Two?

Five?

Did you know the average Jewish family, including sabbaths, observes seventy traditions per year? No wonder they remain resilient in spite of the opposition they have faced through the years.

This tool is perfect for inviting those you are extending your heritage to into your home. Include them in your Christmas or Easter traditions. Let them, maybe for the first time, experience your values through your traditions. Let them discover some traditions are just to celebrate having fun, like annual trips to the coast or mountains. Bring them to your child's baptism or first communion. Help them understand that some traditions establish identity. Show them how to establish a time line for future traditions.

Ray Bohler came to America from Odessa, Russia. Shortly after arriving in the U.S., he and his sister were orphaned. They were tossed from family to family, but Ray survived the customs and lifestyles of a new country. He married and settled into his life's work. He had a call on his life from God to plant churches, and he planted many. The one I presently pastor is one Ray and his wife planted.

Having come to a strange land certainly has its disadvantages, especially when one outlives his family and friends. There were no relatives to care for Ray as he aged. He got lost in the sea of forgetfulness.

My dad, Lloyd Ledbetter, heard one day that Ray was in a home in a city a good distance south of Fresno—our home. He made plans to visit him. Dad's heart was moved by the humbleness of this old gentleman.

He was lonely.

The workers in the home had stolen every possession he had.

He wanted to finish his time here on earth at one of the churches he started.

All he really had was some clothes, his Bible with his churches' charter members' names signed on the front page, and a worn out cassette player to listen to some old sermon tapes.

Dad decided he would extend his heritage to this old warrior of the cross. Ray was now ninety-three. Dad was eighty. Extending your heritage, you see, doesn't have any age barriers.

Dad moved him to Fresno. Took care of his Social Security and SSI income. He didn't put Ray in another home. He leased an apartment in a secured community and hired someone to care for him. Gail and I would have Ray to our house during some of our traditions, like Thanksgiving and Christmas. Others in the church helped him establish some traditions of his own. An old man who thought he had lost his identity found, through a few traditions that we extended to him, that he had an identity after all.

Ray died a few years ago. He was ninety-six.

My dad is eighty-eight now and not doing so well with his health. Many times when I am visiting with my dad I remember his act of extending his heritage to that old gentleman from Russia. When I say something to him about it he just smiles. And I'm reminded again how great this extending thing really is![4]

Family Moments

For extending your heritage, this could be the easiest tool to use. It allows you to seize teachable moments. A teachable moment is that moment that may happen accidentally or intentionally that can be seized and frozen in time by making a memory. Jesus was the master of this tool. The wind blowing reminded Him to teach on the Holy Spirit. A stone was used to teach on the bread of His Word. A death to teach on the resurrection.

Family nights are a perfect place to pass your values. Don't be reluctant to invite others to your family nights. Include a single parent and his or her children. If you are a grandparent, begin to plan family nights for your grandchildren or other children in the neighborhood who haven't experienced this phenomenon.

A friend of Gail and mine has his family nights religously every Monday evening. He never misses. A widow at his church found out what good the family nights were doing his children and approached him and his wife about her daughter. Seems the girl was making some wrong choices. So Jerry and Janice invited this girl to participate in their family nights.

Not long ago Jerry received a letter from the mother. He called me and read it to me. It contained a testimony from the girl, pouring out her heart in thanks to Jerry and Janice for extending a part of their family heritage to her. He told me, "Otis, I have chill bumps all over me." They are thrilled about what extending their heritage to this girl did for her. The beauty of it is, that it seemed to do more for Jerry and Janice than her.

I meet families in every city and church I speak in that have invited a single-parent family to share in their family nights. I meet grandparents who live far from their grandkids, extending their heritage through family nights to neighborhood kids or church family children. Those family nights can be as simple as going out for ice cream to having a planned night with object lessons as teaching agents.[5]

Bottom Line

I want to summarize this chapter by quoting from *Your Heritage*. It articulates our sentiments so well. Why not let it say what needs to be said at this juncture.

> *The Extended Heritage is the process of sharing your heritage with those who may not have a strong heritage of their own.*
>
> *Those who have discovered and mastered the art of giving a strong heritage should extend that blessing to others. It is a wonderful gift that should be shared, not hoarded. And as we've discovered, when you give it, you get even more in return. As Jesus taught, "Give, and it will be given to you. A good measure, pressed down, shaken together and running over, will be poured into your lap. For with the measure you use, it will be measured to you" (Luke 6:38). Practice the art of giving a heritage to those outside your family, and watch this promise of receiving transpire. The blessing will come back at you in many terrific, unexpected ways.[6]*

→ *Chapter 6* ←

Finding, Knowing, and Giving What It Takes

Watching an accomplished musician, artist, speaker, woodworker, or mechanic will most times make us walk away thinking, "That looks so easy. I could do that." Their expertise, their ease of motion, their quick and accurate workmanship makes us forget that it took hours upon hours of honing and practicing their skill to make it look that easy. When we then sit down to learn the same skill, we realize how difficult that particular discipline is and how easy it is not.

Do we have a similar mindset when it comes to our response to children? When we see children who are particularly polite and courteous, when they obey immediately, when children easily engage adults in meaningful conversation without back talk it's easy to say, "Well, must be nice to be a genetically compliant child."

Adults sometimes become confused by the unpredictable behavior of kids, and, instead of making a connection with that child or teen, they will tend to criticize or at best simply ignore him. Oddly enough, that leaves the child or adolescent with a feeling that most adults don't care to try to connect. It's easy for adults to sit back, watch, condemn, and figure out what ails the younger generation, especially when the child or teen's upbringing is not our responsibility. But when we adults make pointing out oversights and suggesting good behavior our responsibility, the playing field no longer looks level. The reality of it doesn't fit our personally perceived blueprint for raising children. It just doesn't work like we thought.

Perhaps it's like Charlie Shedd writes in his book *Promises to Peter*. He says the title of his message on raising children changed with his experience of fatherhood. In his early years on the speaking circuit, before he was a father, he called his message "How to Raise Your Children." People came in droves to hear it. Then Charlie had a child, and it was a while before he gave that message again. When he did, it had a new name: "Some Suggestions to Parents." Two more children and a number of years later, he was calling it "Feeble Hints to Fellow Strugglers." Several years and children later, he seldom gave that talk, but when he did, his theme was, "Anyone Here Got a Few Words of Wisdom."[1]

Some risk-taking adults make connecting with children or teens look easy. They stop and talk to teens in the mall. They

. . . . .

Be Like Jesus

When I was nineteen and not sure where I stood with God, He sent a wonderful family into my life. They treated me as one of their own, never condemning but nourishing me. Eventually I came back to God because of their influence. The woman had epilepsy, and she was ridiculed at work when she passed out. She never retaliated, but always showed each person love. I asked her why. She said if Jesus paid such a high price with His life, it was nothing to be kind to others. She reminded me I need to keep Jesus as my focus.

N.P., San Benito, TX

. . . . .

wave at them in the neighborhood. They encourage neighborhood kids to do well in school or sports. They send birthday cards with well wishes or even invite them to a family backyard barbecue. It looks so easy when they do it. But a simple conversation with them will tell you it wasn't necessarily easy, that it takes time, thoughtful effort, and work. Like Dr. James Dobson's book title says, *Parenting Isn't for Cowards*. I don't presume to be on the same level of expertise that Dr. Dobson is, but may I take some literary license and say, extending your heritage to someone beyond your family isn't for cowards either.

PRINCIPLE: Extending your heritage will take risk, effort, and know-how.

INTENTIONAL IMPACT: To help the extender with resources that will give courage, knowledge, and motivation to accomplish the task.

Now that I've Decided, What Do I Do?

In chapter five, we invited you to take some appropriate steps to choose a lucky person who would have a part in receiving a heritage from you—someone who has not received or is not presently receiving one of her own. Someone who is not likely to receive one if someone like you does not step forward and invite him or her to enjoy yours. This invitation may be either overt or covert in nature. Some you engage will be aware of your efforts and some will not. Nevertheless, let us encourage you to move forward in either case.

The question most often asked about extending your heritage after the obvious "How do I get started?" is, "What do I do now that I have chosen someone to share my legacies with?"

It would be nice if there were a handbook with specific instructions and directions as to how to effect a successful transfer of our heritage. One where we could follow step one that will lead to step two, and so on until every step is exhausted and success is achieved. Something like putting a train set together on Christmas Eve, so we could step back with thumbs in our vests and swell with immediate gratification, bursting with pride.

That may be true in a place Dorothy calls Oz, but it "ain't so" in a place called Reality.

The Power of Values

At the risk of being politically incorrect and the chance of being criticized, we want to go against the cultural mindset concerning fixing what ails our youth. There are those who think if the government will just throw just a little more money at education, the sinking boat of morals may stay afloat.

If that scenario is valid, then why don't we throw a bag of money to a drowning man instead of a life ring? Or why don't we give a person dying of a tragic disease a few more greenbacks? Could it be because while education is good in itself, it is not the answer?

Others say midnight basketball . . . still others want gun control, or legislation and incarceration for hate crimes. All of those suggested solutions, while having some merit by themselves, are nothing more than societal gauze used to cover a wound that is smothered by benign emotional salve. Doesn't the notion that a change of mind and increased revenue will fix our sickness miss the mark by about eighteen inches? Perhaps we need to lower our sights and aim at the heart. A change of heart is the only solution, and the heart only changes when values are honored.

There Is Help

While discussing the importance of this book with my co-author, Randy Scott, he shared some wonderful information with me. I opened the stapled booklet he handed me and began to read. It took only seconds for the significance of the material to soak in. What I was reading was almost like a handbook. At least it was the closest thing we have ever seen to one, so we asked permission to share it with you. (If you want more data concerning this survey, refer to the information about the Search Institute in the endnotes, page 156).

In their own words, "Search Institute has identified some building blocks of healthy development that help young people grow up healthy, caring, and responsible. Percentages of young people who experience each asset represent almost 100,000 6th to 12th-grade youth surveyed in 213 towns and cities in the United States."[2]

If you are like us you will read quickly through the following list. We admit we did too, because we were excited about the possibilities for parents present and future. But let us admonish each of you to take your time. Let this information drown your distractions and saturate your appetite for success.

40 Developmental Assets

CATEGORY   **ASSET NAME AND DEFINITION**

• Support
    1. Family support—Family life provides high levels of love and support.
    2. Positive family communication—Young person and her or his parent(s) communicate positively, and young person is willing to seek advice and counsel from parent(s).
    3. Other adult relationships—Young person receives support from three or more non-parent adults.
    4. Caring neighborhood—Young person experiences caring neighbors.
    5. Caring school climate—School provides a caring, encouraging environment.

6. Parent involvement in schooling—Parent(s) are actively involved in helping young person succeed in school.

- Empowerment
    7. Community values youth—Young person perceives that adults in the community value youth.
    8. Youth as resources—Young people are given useful roles in the community.
    9. Service to others—Young person serves in the community one hour or more per week.
    10. Safety—Young person feels safe at home, at school, and in the neighborhood.

- Boundaries & Expectations
    11. Family boundaries—Family has clear rules and consequences and monitors the young person's whereabouts.
    12. School boundaries—School provides clear rules and consequences.
    13. Neighborhood boundaries—Neighbors take responsibility for monitoring young people's behavior.
    14. Adult role models—Parent(s) and other adults model positive, responsible behavior.
    15. Positive peer influence—Young person's best friends model responsible behavior.
    16. High expectations—Both parent(s) and teachers encourage the young person to do well.

- Constructive Use of Time
    17. Creative activities—Young person spends three or more hours per week in lessons or practice in music, theater, or other arts.
    18. Youth programs—Young person spends three or more hours per week in sports, clubs, or organizations at school and/or in the community.

19. Religious community—Young person spends one or more hours per week in activities in a religious institution.
20. Time at home—Young person is out with friends "with nothing special to do" two or fewer nights per week.

- Commitment to Learning
  21. Achievement motivation—Young person is motivated to do well in school.
  22. School engagement—Young person is actively engaged in learning.
  23. Homework—Young person reports doing at least one hour of homework every school day
  24. Bonding to school—Young person cares about her or his school.
  25. Reading for pleasure—Young person reads for pleasure three or more hours per week.

- Positive Values
  26. Caring—Young person places high value on helping other people.
  27. Equality and social justice—Young person places high value on promoting equality and reducing hunger and poverty.
  28. Integrity—Young person acts on convictions and stands up for her or his beliefs.
  29. Honesty—Young person tells the truth even when it is not easy.
  30. Responsibility—Young person accepts and takes personal responsibility.

· · · · ·

Second Mother

My mother-in-law was my "second" mother during my teen years. I didn't even know her son until my last year-and-a-half of high school. My mother-in-law has always given me courage and hope that God is almighty and that He loves me.

K.S. Frostburg, MD

· · · · ·

31. Restraint—Young person believes it is important not to be sexually active or to use alcohol or other drugs.

- Social Competencies
    32. Planning and decision making—Young person knows how to plan ahead and make choices.
    33. Interpersonal competence—Young person has empathy, sensitivity and friendship skills.
    34. Cultural competence—Young person has knowledge of and comfort with people of different cultural/racial/ethnic backgrounds.
    35. Resistance skills—Young person can resist negative peer pressure and dangerous situations.
    36. Peaceful conflict resolution—Young person seeks to resolve conflict nonviolently.

- Positive Identity
    37. Personal power—Young person feels he or she has control over "things that happen to me."
    38. Self-esteem—Young person reports having a high self-esteem.
    39. Sense of purpose—Young person reports that "my life has a purpose."
    40. Positive view of personal future—Young person is optimistic about her or his personal future.[3]

A Glowing Report for Values _____

The Search Institute survey found that the forty assets listed above powerfully protect youth from a wide variety of risky behaviors. In fact, their information showed that the more of these assets the youth experienced the less likely he or she would participate in risky behavior.

Study the following chart.

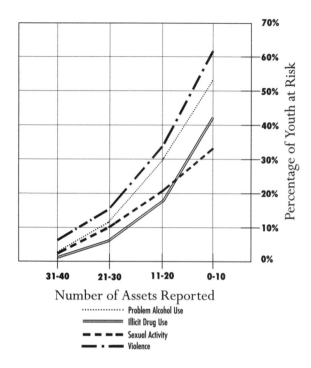

Number of Assets Reported

.... Problem Alcohol Use
━━━━━ Illicit Drug Use
▬ ▬ ▬ Sexual Activity
━ ▪ ━ Violence

The problem is that our youth have far too few of the forty assets surrounding their lives. It's as if they have no foundation, or at best, a weak one. Search Institute, that released this survey, suggests the best-case scenario is that all kids should have at least thirty-one of the forty assets. Yet the truth is, only 8 percent ever reach that goal. Their finding reveals

20% have	0 – 10	assets
42% have	11 – 20	assets
30% have	21 – 30	assets
8% have	31 – 40	assets

That means 62 percent of surveyed youths have fewer than 20 of these assets.

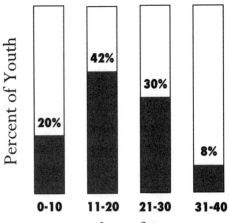

Number of Assets

Making a List, Checking It Twice _____

Information is powerful! Information begs the recipient to act and not allow it to lay dormant. Information unused is like buying a car only to occupy your garage. The knowledge that you have it doesn't get you anywhere. It's just an admirable and potentially powerful item to have filling empty space. Now that information is available to help us increase the odds for our children's survival, what will we do with it?

You may be feeling overwhelmed at the amount of information contained in the list of forty assets. Of course there aren't many people who will commit all the information to memory, so don't despair. Memorization isn't really even needed at this point, but awareness is.

> .....
>
> ### Planting Seeds
>
> My mother worked in the church nursery for thirty-five years planting seeds among others, in addition to raising her own family. When she left this world she did not leave us wealth as far as the world counts wealth. But for eternity she left wealth untold.
>
> J.L. Warrenton, MO
>
> .....

Did the above list raise your awareness as to the subject matter that you are extending beyond your family? Does the list help bring ideas into your mind as to how you may be more creative in extending your heritage? Perhaps you will want to read the forty particulars again, and this time read slower and more deliberately. Concentrate on the ones you are doing well. Try remembering them for the checklist.

After re-reading the list, now work the checklist below. Put a check mark in the box to the left of each one you are teaching well, leaving the ones blank that might need improvement. Have the child/teen you presently work with complete the checklist also.

Now compare your tallies. This will give you an idea of the areas you will want to have conversations about. The checklist appears just as it does in the Search Institute material.

An Asset Checklist _____

Many people find it helpful to use a simple checklist to reflect on the assets young people experience. This checklist simplifies the asset list to help prompt conversation in families, organizations, and communities. NOTE: This checklist is not intended nor appropriate as a scientific or accurate measurement of developmental assets.

☐ 1. I receive high levels of love and support from family members.

☐ 2. I can go to my parent(s) or guardian(s) for advice and support and have frequent, in-depth conversations with them.

☐ 3. I know some non-parent adults I can go to for advice and support.

☐ 4. My neighbors encourage and support me.

☐ 5. My school provides a caring, encouraging environment.

☐ 6. My parent(s) or guardian(s) help me succeed in school.

☐ 7. I feel valued by adults in my community.

☐ 8. I am given useful roles in my community.

☐ 9. I serve in the community one hour or more each week.

☐ 10. I feel safe at home, at school, and in the neighborhood.

☐ 11. My family sets standards for appropriate conduct and monitors my whereabouts.

☐ 12. My school has clear rules and consequences for behavior.

☐ 13. Neighbors take responsibility for monitoring my behavior.

☐ 14. Parent(s) and other adults model positive, responsible behavior.

☐ 15. My best friends model responsible behavior.

☐ 16. My parent(s)/guardian(s) and teachers encourage me to do well.

☐ 17. I spend three hours or more each week in lessons or practice in music, theater, or other arts.

☐ 18. I spend three hours or more each week in school or community sports, clubs, or organizations.

☐ 19. I spend one hour or more each week in religious services or participating in spiritual activities.

☐ 20. I go out with friends "with nothing special to do" two or fewer nights each week.

☐ 21. I want to do well in school.

☐ 22. I am actively engaged in learning.

☐ 23. I do an hour or more of homework each school day.

☐ 24. I care about my school.

☐ 25. I read for pleasure three or more hours each week.

☐ 26. I believe it is really important to help other people.

☐ 27. I want to help promote equality and reduce world poverty and hunger.

☐ 28. I can stand up for what I believe.

☐ 29. I tell the truth even when it's not easy.

☐ 30. I can accept and take personal responsibility.

☐ 31. I believe it is important not to be sexually active or to use alcohol or other drugs.

☐ 32. I am good at planning ahead and making decisions.

☐ 33. I am good at making and keeping friends.

☐ 34. I know and am comfortable with people of different cultural/racial/ethnic backgrounds.

☐ 35. I can resist negative peer pressure and dangerous situations.

☐ 36. I try to resolve conflict non-violently.

☐ 37. I believe I have control over many things that happen to me.

☐ 38. I feel good about myself.

☐ 39. I believe my life has a purpose.

☐ 40. I am optimistic about my future.[4]

A Plan of Action _____

Our desire is that you will become intentional about extending your heritage. We at Heritage Builders Association know that it doesn't happen by accident. So the following is a worksheet for organizing your plan of action. With a pencil, place in each space the asset from the previous list in order of your priority with the number corresponding to it. We realize some of the assets may already be a part of your family or extended family. Excellent! List them last on your chart. Certainly you will want to reinforce them as the child or teen grows.

If you are extending your heritage beyond your family, make a separate list for those you are influencing. If they come from dysfunctional families, or have simply chosen you as an adult they trust to coach them, their list may have different priorities than those in your family. So choose carefully and prayerfully for each person.

Prioritized List _____

1. _____	2. _____	3. _____	4. _____
5. _____	6. _____	7. _____	8. _____
9. _____	10. _____	11. _____	12. _____
13. _____	14. _____	15. _____	16. _____
17. _____	18. _____	19. _____	20. _____
21. _____	22. _____	23. _____	24. _____

25. _____   26. _____   27. _____   28. _____

29. _____   30. _____   31. _____   32. _____

33. _____   34. _____   35. _____   36. _____

37. _____   38. _____   39. _____   40. _____

After you have prioritized your thoughts from the forty assets, it's time to arrange them on the following calendar. Since there are fifty-two weeks in the year and only forty assets we recommend that you first put an X in the space representing the weeks you will be on vacation and those weeks you will take as holidays. (There will be one extra week per month more than the number of assets.) If you prefer not to X out twelve weeks, then you may want to identify the assets to which you will give extra attention using them twice in a year. Either way, begin to list the assets by the prioritized number in the spaces below.

(Example: If number 1 on your prioritized list is asset number 24, then 24 will be placed in the first space of the month you decide to begin.)

If you are beginning in a month other than January you will want to make the month you begin contain those assets you have prioritized highest.

Although we understand most months only have four weeks, it changes from year to year, so we provided an extra space in each month to accommodate those months that have five weeks in them.

Now that you have prioritized, begin to fill in the spaces that correspond with the week and month you intend to intentionally communicate a particular asset.

Prioritized Calendar _____

Jan.	__ __ __ __ __	July	__ __ __ __ __
Feb.	__ __ __ __ __	Aug.	__ __ __ __ __
Mar.	__ __ __ __ __	Sept.	__ __ __ __ __
April	__ __ __ __ __	Oct.	__ __ __ __ __
May	__ __ __ __ __	Nov.	__ __ __ __ __
June	__ __ __ __ __	Dec.	__ __ __ __ __

As we said at the first of this chapter, when an artist makes his trade look easy, we go away saying, "I can do that." We know the process of extending a heritage is not an easy one. Our hopes are that it now seems easier. The need has been exposed. The tools have been explained. The path to the process has been mapped, now all that is needed is you. Many are out there in our churches, schools, and neighborhoods, waiting for us to risk reaching out.

Have a wonderful time with those to whom you have chosen to pass your heritage. Great will be your reward here and beyond!

It Just So Happened _____

My (J.Otis) secretary and her husband have been helping me put the finishing touches on this chapter. They helped me simplify the wording by reading the plan of action section and pointing out where the process of charting a prioritized list bogged down. It has made the manuscript become much more understandable.

During this time a curious phone call came into the church office. It was from a woman who has been attending the church for a while. She asked if she could meet with me. Her voice had urgency in it so the appointment was set during the lunch hour today.

It lasted an hour.

I just returned to this keyboard that has been my mistress for several months now. She and I are practically inseparable. But for this separation during lunch, I am thankful, because I came face to face with the very reason I wanted to write this book. I'll explain.

The lady, I will call her Carrie, began her conversation with me, "My three kids and I have a saying around our house about your book *Your Heritage*."

"What's that?" I asked, expecting to hear perhaps a compliment.

But she told me, "We say with sarcasm, 'Oh, what a heritage!'"

She searched my eyes for a response. I was taken aback. I really didn't know what to say. Then she continued.

I learned that her husband is an addict, a loser who is likely going to prison. She already has told him if he goes to prison again (he's been there twice), she and the kids won't be there when he gets out.

"I don't think a decent man exists," she snapped. "Present company excepted," she added quickly staring at me with a grin. But the smile was fleeting. Her countenance dropped as she told me more, "My father, the pervert, abused me, so I got married to escape that and I got this."

It's at times like this when the ministry is difficult.

. . . . .

To the Fifth Generation

My extended family includes over 100 people who are followers of Christ as a result of my great grandparents' conversion nearly a century ago. The legacy continues in its fifth generation today. I am so grateful for the spiritual heritage that has allowed me to experience the love and power of God and the thrill of passing the faith to future generations.

K.S. Ypsilanti, MI

. . . . .

What do I say to a lady at a time like this? I hunted through my memory to come up with something.

Nothing!

Silence!

A deafening stillness!

Her plans are to separate, find an apartment she can afford, and do whatever she has to, to make it.

"I didn't get a good heritage," Carrie remarked. Her eyes don't let mine look away. I wait for her next comment. "I want my kids to have one, but now I'm not sure if that will ever happen."

It was then that I realized God had put her in my path at this very moment for a very specific reason.

"J.Otis!" I shouted to myself. "Focus! . . . This is what you are writing about."

As I walked away from that meeting I told myself that I am going to make it my ministry to find a family that will extend their heritage to this woman and her three kids. Gail and I already have two families we are extending toward. But there are others out there eager to get involved. Someone to learn the forty assets and help Carrie prioritize them and establish them in her kids' lives. I want to see all three of them fall into that 31–40 category. I want them to have every chance, without exception, that every kid should have.

Look back at whom God has brought into your life. Maybe it's someone you have heretofore overlooked. Maybe it is another Carrie similar to the one I met today.

Could this be our opportunity?

Could we be angels unaware?

→ Chapter 7 ←

Extending Your Heritage Success Stories

*H*ow does one measure success? I (J. Otis) have participated in many strategic planning sessions where this question is asked. At some meetings the question is answered to the satisfaction of those present, and in others the answer alludes everyone.

Parenting and mentoring in the extended family is a good place to pose this question. No one wants to fail in these efforts, yet we see families disintegrating all around us. We see children, teens, and sadly, even adults, trying to find their way through the maze of maturing without any life model to build upon. These are the ones who need someone to step forward and say as the Apostle Paul said to his extended family member Timothy, "Follow me as I follow God."

Olivia's Story

In our book *Your Heritage*, Kurt Bruner and I gave illustrations on what it is like to have someone extend his or her heritage to you. Kurt has first-hand information as he describes briefly what tran-

· · · · ·

Christ at Center

One reason we became members of our present church was the example of a family we had developed a friendship with. They have Christ at the center of all they do. The husband and wife have passed it on to their children and its effects are obvious. Not having had this kind of spiritual heritage from my family, I thank the Lord for this godly family's example.

R.T.M. Brooklyn, NY

· · · · ·

spired in the life of his wife, Olivia.

If you want to observe a success story in action, you should meet Olivia. She is one of those people who attracts others to herself like a magnet. She has the gift of encouragement, and she uses it. And yet, if anyone has reason to feel discouraged, it is Olivia. She was given a weak heritage—spiritually, emotionally, and relationally. Hers was a childhood of neglect, rejection, and pain. But she has overcome the past and is building a wonderful heritage for her own family today.

Growing up in a single-parent home with five siblings would have been difficult enough for Olivia. Adding to the stress, she watched as her four brothers and sister dealt with the ongoing fallout of family collapse—memories of Daddy hitting Mommy, the confusion, the fear, the rejection, several serious bouts with suicide-level depression, and one attempt to actually carry out the suicide compulsion.

Olivia had little time with her mother, who was working days and attending school in the evenings. There was no time, money, or energy to braid her hair, buy pretty party dresses, or talk about boys. Even when they were together, there was more shouting than sharing. Of course, there was no healthy male role model in the home. No one to call her "daddy's little sweetheart" or teach her to ride that first bicycle.

Olivia was given no positive spiritual heritage. Olivia's mother had rejected her Catholic roots. Her emotional and social legacy was weak. Home was a place to fight, not a place to rest.

Olivia understands the value of what we've labeled "the extended heritage." She received it from two families during critical periods of her own life. They gave her something she would have never otherwise received—a glimpse of what a heritage can be and an understanding of how to give what she hadn't received at home . . . which, by the way, is the essence of our definition. Put simply . . .

The "extended heritage" is the process of sharing your heritage with those who may not have a strong heritage of their own.[1]

Recording Artist Paula Dunn in Her Own Words

Although many people's heritage centers on the family they were born into, not everyone has the experience of being raised by their biological mom and dad. Divorce, sickness, abuse, and even death can ravage families, leaving people broken, weak, and at best, functioning by rote. However, even in the midst of bleak circumstances, God can work a plan. A plan that can be traced through willing people that He uses to carry out His purposes. And thus begins my story . . .

When I was six weeks old, my father was imprisoned and my mom was bedridden with three children to take care of. My brother was two, and my sister was four. A husband and wife were on church visitation one day in our city just randomly choosing houses to visit. Nobody told them to come to our house, but that day they did. They saw our need, and assured my mom that they wanted to help her in any way. Since she did not know what else to do, she allowed me, as the baby, to go and live with this family until she got better. For the next few years, I lived between both families. When my dad got out of prison, there was a lot of fighting, drinking, drugs, abuse, etc.— essentially a very unhappy home. The family from the church, however, gave me much love and taught me about God and His love. In fact, they were the ones who led me to the Lord at the young age of four.

When I reached school age, the family from the church paid the tuition to put me into a Christian school. I then proceeded to live with them during the week and with my real parents on weekends, clearly reinforcing the difference between a Christ-centered home and one in desperate need of Him.

When I was eight, my mom developed cancer. She died three painful years later. Shortly after my mom's death, my dad kicked first my sister and then my brother out of the house when they each turned fourteen. I then stayed with the family from the church permanently. My dad didn't much care either way.

My brother and sister have had much heartache and have made many wrong choices. I know if it weren't for God's intervening in my life that would be my story also. My brother has tried the drug and alcohol scene and has been in and out of jail. My sister has bounced from relationship to relationship and finally thought she found happiness. She got married and six months later was divorced. She is still searching today.

Practically every day when I awaken, I thank God for what He has done and saved me from in my life. My heart also overflows with gratitude to the most powerful examples of Jesus that I have ever seen—Joe and Gloria Young, the family that took me in. You see, the story wasn't just for me. It was part of an even greater Master Plan. This wonderful couple had always wanted a daughter. They had three boys when they found out they could not have any more children. They were very disappointed and began to consider adopting a girl. They found a little Indian girl that they fell in love with and began the process. At the last visit, the adoption fell through. They gave up on their dream of having a little girl and focused exclusively on raising their three boys and working within their local church.

Years later they were transferred to Maine. Their boys graduated from school, got married, and began having families of their own. It was at this point in their lives that they found me and got involved in my young life, never dreaming that they would end up becoming my parents.

It's amazing to think of what could have happened if they had decided that they were too busy to go on visitation that night, or that my family was too complicated to get involved with. God knew exactly what He was doing, and even used my life to be a blessing to them.

My high school years are filled with many warm memories that I will forever cherish. It was during the next few years that they carted me around to sing in different churches throughout New England. A music ministry that my husband and I now do full time developed as a result of those concerts. Every decision that is made, and every life that is changed is a direct result of the Youngs taking the time out of their lives to touch and impact my life forever. Some day there will be people in heaven because of what this selfless couple did in my life.

My relationship with these wonderful parents is very close. I can never thank or love them enough for what they have done

> · · · · ·
> ### *Homeschooling*
>
> I can't tell you how challenged I have been by other homeschooling families that I know or have read about. The ideas they have shared about the spiritual training of their children have inspired me and given me a vision to continue training and discipline my children.
>
> *D.P. Strongsville, OH*
>
> · · · · ·

for me. They didn't have to take me in. They didn't have to love me. They chose to do it—which is exactly what Christ did for us. He didn't have to love or die for us, but He chose to extend his heritage to the human race.

I hope that my life can be an example to others on the value of mentoring, and I look forward to impacting another life as much as mine has been touched.

A Cousin Brought to His Father's Niece

Was it a disease, was it homicide, was it an execution, or was it some other odd circumstance that left young Esther alone? The reader of the book by her name isn't told. Perhaps the reason is that what has happened in her past is not as important as what was going to happen in her future. Perhaps it is because her story was revealed so we would focus on her extended heritage and not the one from her immediate family.

Whatever the case, we are drawn into a compelling story of debauchery, love, beauty, attempted murder, and justice.

Enter the heritage extender, Mordecai. God prepared him and sent him to be a model for Esther. We aren't told if he balked at the responsibility or if he counted it a delight. We are only told that his values were so ingrained in her that when the opportunity arose for her to save her people there was no question as to what her response would be. Her own welfare took a back seat.

She went through risking her life, manipulating the murderous plot of Haman to the good of her people, calling her entire nation to fasting and prayer, and creating a national celebration that is still observed today. What a story of extending influence to your family and beyond. Think of it! A nation brought to the

Father's knees, because a cousin was brought to his father's niece!

A Foster Pastor

Eli wasn't a good father. His hand was far too loose when it came to guiding his two sons Hophni and Phinehas. When they acted up in temple worship he turned a blind eye. When they wanted to be young ministers and do what was right in their own eyes for the people, Dad copped the attitude "boys will be boys." He wasn't even effective in his move against them when he learned they were seducing women at the door of the temple. When he finally did rebuke them, his deafness toward their attitude contaminated his sons' hearing. They took no heed to what he was saying, even though it turned out to be good advice. But what he could not achieve with his blood sons, he was allowed to accomplish with a foster son.

A mother named Hannah gave her son to be influenced by Eli, and Eli didn't fail here. Perhaps by now he had learned from his previous mistakes. Chapter 3 of 1 Samuel opens the private doors of Eli's house and allows us to listen in on a very personal conversation. Eli instructed Samuel correctly. When Samuel heard the voice of God in the night and did not recognize it he went to Eli's bedside and asked advice. "Go back to your bed, when He calls again, tell Him to speak for Your servant is listening." Samuel did! God spoke!

For some reading this book, perhaps you feel you blew it with your children. You wish you could do it over. We have a good word for you. YOU CAN! There are many young boys and girls waiting to be influenced by someone who has learned from his or her mistakes. Take Eli's advice to Samuel, and when He puts a child or teen in your life, tell God, "Speak, Lord, Your servant is listening."

Encouraging Words from our Survey _____

We mailed a survey asking people to "help us compile some of the great ways that you have extended your spiritual heritage outside your immediate family, or how someone has extended their heritage to you or a member of your family." We received a great response. Here are some of the replies in the words of the heritage extenders:

. . . . .

Popsili's Praise

My memories of my grandfather, Popsili, are foundational to what I am. He loved the Lord and to sing praise songs to Him (loudly), whether he could read the words or not.

R.D & E.D, Simi Valley, CA

. . . . .

My dad was an alcoholic and my mother was addicted to my father and amphetamines. Aunt Dixie was my great, great aunt. I lived with her frequently as a small child and teenager. She was a Christian even when no one was looking.

God healed me of leukemia when I was eight. I was told it was terminal and I would never leave the hospital alive. At best, I had three months. Through the prayers of one righteous woman I was healed. I left the hospital seven days later.

Later in life I became a drug addict, mainlining heroin at age fifteen. But I lived next door to a Nazerene Church. The minister's name was Pastor York. He took time with me. He was sweet and gentle, something I never experienced in my house. All I saw there was fights.

I had been molested as far back as I could remember by a family member. When things got real bad, I would slip away to the sanctuary where it was quiet. Frequently Pastor York would find me asleep in or under a pew.

I am sure it was Pastor York and Aunt Dixie's prayers that protected me during the years of addiction and molestation.

These are the only two people I ever saw Jesus in, and in these two, He did shine!

Thank you for asking,

Janet, Evansville, IN

When I became a Christian it was awesome to me to know that I had this whole big church family that would love me and pray with me without any ulterior motives. (As you can guess, I wasn't raised in a Christian home.) These people literally became my family with the Heavenly Father as Father God, Dad of us all.

Debbie, Sterling, CO

Janet was an older lady at our church (about fifteen years older than me). She took it upon herself to be a "Titus" woman to many of the young women at our church. She met with us individually, would find out our needs and struggles, and biblically counseled and discipled us. God used her in my life as a role model. Since my mother had passed away and I was newly married she was able to show me how to be the wife and mother God intended me to be.

Angela, Tucson, AZ

A Sister's Influence

My sister was always close to Jesus, from the time she was a child. I, however, rejected much of the "religiosity" of my upbringing until I went on a retreat with my sister's college fellowship group. I made a commitment to the Lord that weekend, and through my sister's encouragement and belief in me, I grew as a Christian year by year.

K.E. Largo, FL

My friend Teresa left me a legacy of true worship. Hers was a lifestyle of obedience to and adoration of our God. Just watching her worship led me into the throne room of His presence. I hope I will do the same for others.

Belinda, Big Bear Lake, CA

As a small child, I remember sitting on my grandfather's lap under a palm tree where he told me stories of Jesus. Years later I found a picture I had never seen before of him standing in that very spot. In the picture, he is holding a string of fish. How incredible God is! That picture is in our Creative Memory photo album as a part of our spiritual history.

Penny, Muncie, IN

We received so many responses there would be no way to put them all in this book. The number of families who could look back over their history and recall moments in detail where legacies were being passed encouraged us. Some remembered parents, others their grandparents. Some told us of friendships that have changed their lives, while others tell of neighbors, Sunday School teachers, coaches, or a member of their extended family who brought something to them that changed their life. A few of the stories consisted of only a sentence or two. Additional recitals were in detail, long and thorough. Each was making the corresponding point we make in this book. And that point restated is:

It is possible and rewarding to extend your heritage to your family and beyond.

Appendix

SPIRITUAL LEGACY EVALUATION

Answer each question by circling the number that best reflects the legacy you have received from your parents; then add your total score.

1. To what degree were spiritual principles incorporated into daily family life?
　　1–Never
　　2–Rarely
　　3–Sometimes
　　4–Frequently
　　5–Almost always
　　6–Consistently

2. Which word captures the tone of how you learned to view/relate to God?
　　1–Absent
　　2–Adversarial
　　3–Fearful
　　4–Casual
　　5–Solemn
　　6–Intimate

3. How would you summarize your family's level of participation in spiritual activities?
　　1–Nonexistent
　　2–Rare

3–Occasional
4–Regimental
5–Active
6–Enthusiastic

4. How were spiritual discussions applied in your home?
1–They weren't
2–To control
3–To manipulate
4–To teach
5–To influence
6–To reinforce

5. What was the perspective in your home with regard to moral absolutes?
1–If it feels good, do it!
2–There are no absolutes
3–Let your heart guide you
4–Legalistic rules
5–Conservative values
6–Clear life boundaries

Results

Above 24	=	Strong spiritual legacy
19-24	=	Healthy legacy
14-18	=	Mixed legacy—good and bad elements
10-13	=	Weak spiritual legacy
Below 10	=	Damaged spiritual legacy

EMOTIONAL LEGACY EVALUATION

Answer each question by circling the number that best reflects the legacy you have received from your parents; then add your total score.

1. When you walked into your house, what was your feeling?
1–Dread
2–Tension
3–Chaos
4–Stability
5–Calm
6–Warmth

2. Which word best describes the tone of your home?
   1–Hateful
   2–Angry
   3–Sad
   4–Serious
   5–Relaxed
   6–Fun

3. What was the message of your family life?
   1–You are worthless.
   2–You are a burden.
   3–You are OK.
   4–You are respected.
   5–You are important.
   6–You are the greatest.

4. Which word best describes the "fragrance" of your home life?
   1–Repulsive
   2–Rotten
   3–Unpleasant
   4–Sterile
   5–Fresh
   6–Sweet

5. Which was most frequent in your home?
   1–An intense fight
   2–The silent treatment
   3–Detached apathy
   4–A strong disagreement
   5–A kind word
   6–An affectionate hug

Results

Above 24	= Strong emotional legacy
19-24	= Healthy legacy
14-18	= Mixed legacy—good and bad elements
10-13	= Weak emotional legacy
Below 10	= Damaged emotional legacy

SOCIAL LEGACY EVALUATION

Answer each question by circling the number that best reflects the legacy you have received from your parents; then add your total score.

1. Which words most closely resemble the social tone of your family?
    1–Cruel and abusive
    2–Cutting sarcasm
    3–Chaotic and distant
    4–Noncommunicative but stable
    5–Secure with open communcation
    6–Loving and fun

2. What was the message of your home life with regard to relationships?
    1–"Step on others to get your way."
    2–"Hurt them if they hurt you."
    3–"Demand your rights."
    4–"Mind your own business."
    5–"Treat others with respect."
    6–"Put others before yourself."

3. How were rules set and enforced in your home?
    1–Independent of relationship
    2–In reaction to parental stress
    3–Dictatorially
    4–Inconsistently
    5–Out of concern for my well-being
    6–In the context of a loving relationship

4. Which word best characterizes the tone of communication in your home?
    1–Shouting
    2–Manipulation
    3–Confusing
    4–Clear
    5–Constructive
    6–Courteous

5. How did your family deal with wrong behavior?

1–Subtle reinforcement
2–Accepted in the name of love
3–Guilt trip
4–Severe punishment
5–Discussion
6–Loving, firm discipline

Results

Above 24	=	Strong social legacy
19-24	=	Healthy legacy
14-18	=	Mixed legacy—good and bad elements
10-13	=	Weak social legacy
Below 10	=	Damaged social legacy

How to Lead Your Child to Christ

Some things to consider ahead of time:

1. Realize that God is more concerned about your child's eternal destiny and happiness than you are. "The Lord is not slow in keeping his promise. . . . He is patient with you, not wanting anyone to perish, but everyone to come to repentance" (2 Peter 3:9).

2. Pray specifically beforehand that God will give you insights and wisdom in dealing with each child on his or her maturity level.

3. Don't use terms like "take Jesus into your heart," "dying and going to hell," and "accepting Christ as your personal Savior." Children are either too literal ("How does Jesus breathe in my heart?") or the words are too clichéd and trite for their understanding.

4. Deal with each child alone, and don't be in a hurry. Make sure he or she understands. Discuss. Take your time. A few cautions:

1. When drawing children to Himself, Jesus said for others to "allow" them to come to Him (see Mark 10:14). Only with adults did He use the term "compel" (see Luke 14:23). Do not compel children.

2. Remember that unless the Holy Spirit is speaking to the child, there will be no genuine heart experience of regeneration. Parents, don't get caught up in the idea that Jesus will return the day before you were going to speak to your child about salvation and that it will be too late. Look at God's character-He is love! He is not dangling your child's soul over hell. Wait on God's timing. Pray with faith, believing. Be concerned, but don't push.

The Plan:

1. God loves you. Recite John 3:16 with your child's name in place of "the world."

2. Show the child his or her need of a Savior.

a. Deal with sin carefully. There is one thing that can not enter heaven—sin.

b. Be sure your child knows what sin is. Ask him to name some (things common to children—lying, sassing, disobeying, etc.). Sin is doing or thinking anything wrong according to God's Word. It is breaking God's Law.

c. Ask the question "Have you sinned?" If the answer is no, do not continue. Urge him to come and talk to you again when he does feel that he has sinned. Dismiss him. You may want to have prayer first, however, thanking God "for this young child who is willing to do what is right." Make it easy for him to talk to you again, but do not continue. Do not say, "Oh, yes, you have too sinned!" and then name some. With children, wait for God's conviction.

d. If the answer is yes, continue. He may even give a personal illustration of some sin he has done recently or one that has bothered him.

e. Tell him what God says about sin: We've all sinned ("There is no one righteous, not even one," Rom. 3:10). And because of that sin, we can't get to God ("For the wages of sin is death . . . " Rom. 6:23). So He had to come to us (". . . but the gift of God is eternal life in Christ Jesus our Lord," Rom. 6:23).

f. Relate God's gift of salvation to Christmas gifts-we don't earn them or pay for them; we just accept them and are thankful for them.

3. Bring the child to a definite decision.

a. Christ must be received if salvation is to be possessed.

b. Remember, do not force a decision.

c. Ask the child to pray out loud in her own words. Give her some things she could say if she seems unsure. Now be prepared for a blessing! (It is best to avoid having the child repeat a memorized prayer after you. Let her think, and make it personal.)*

d. After salvation has occurred, pray for her out loud. This is a good way to pronounce a blessing on her.

4. Lead your child into assurance. Show him that he will have to keep his relationship open with God through repentance and forgiveness (just like with his family or friends), but that God will always love him ("Never will I leave you; never will I forsake you," Heb. 13:5).

* If you wish to guide your child through the prayer, here is some suggested language.

"Dear God, I know that I am a sinner [have child name specific sins he or she acknowledged earlier, such as lying, stealing, disobeying, etc.]. I know that Jesus died on the cross to pay for all my sins. I ask You to forgive me of my sins. I believe that Jesus died for me and rose from the dead, and I accept Him as my Savior. Thank You for loving me. In Jesus' name. Amen."

Sources

BIBLE LEARNING CD-ROMS

Scripture Sleuth – New Testament and Old Testament Trivia
  Ages 9-90 (Ideal/Instructional Fair)
The Baker Bible Encyclopedia
  Ages 8-12 (Baker)
Bibleland.com
  Ages 8-12 (Baker)
New Kids Point and Play Bible
  Ages 8-12 (Baker)
The Amazing Expedition Bible
  Ages 8-12 (Baker)
Illustrated Manners and Customs of the Bible
  (Thomas Nelson)
Baker Bible Dictionary for Kids
  Ages 5-8 (Baker)
Baker Book of Bible People for Kids
  Ages 5-8 (Baker)
The Baker Bible Handbook for Kids
  Ages 8-12 (Baker)
The Children's Bible Encyclopedia
  Ages 8+ (Baker)

BIBLES

The New Testament Picture Bible
  Ages 8+ (David C. Cook/Chariot Victor)

The Picture Bible
Ages 8-12 (David C. Cook/Chariot Victor)
Psalty's Kids Bible
Ages 4-8 (Zondervan)
Precious Moments Bible
Out of print
New Explorers Study Bible
Ages 7-12 (Thomas Nelson)
The New Adventures Bible
Ages 8-12 (Zondervan)
Life Application Bible
Ages 8-12 (Tyndale)
The One Year Bible for Kids
Ages 8-12 (Tyndale)
Step-By-Step Bible
Ages 8-12 (David C. Cook/Chariot Victor)

DEVOTIONALS
Spending Prime Time With God Series
Ages 10-12 (Broadman & Holman)
Frogs in Pharaoh's Bed
Ages 6-11 (Tyndale)
Caution: Dangerous Devotions
Ages 8+ (Chariot Victor)
The Children's Daily Devotional Bible
Ages 6-11 (Thomas Nelson)
Daily Bread for Boys and Girls
Ages 6-12 (Child Evangelism)
Picture Bible Devotions
Ages 8-12 (Chariot Victor)
Kids' Book of Decisions
Ages 7-11 (Zondervan)
The One Year Book of Family Devotions, Vol 1-3
Ages 2+ (Tyndale)
Little Visits Every Day
Ages 4-7 (Concordia)
Little Visits With God
Ages 7-10 (Concordia)

Little Visits With Jesus
  Ages 4-7 (Concordia)
Little Visits For Toddlers
  Ages 0-3 (Concordia)
Little Visits For Families
  Ages 7-10 (Concordia)
Sticky Situations
  Ages 8-12 (Tyndale)
The One Year Book of Devotions for Kids, Vol. 1-3
  Ages 2+ (Tyndale)
Family Walk
  Ages 10+ (Walk Thru the Bible)
I Want to Know Series
  Ages 7-10 (Zondervan)
Devotions from the World of Sports
  Ages 8+ (David C. Cook/Chariot Victor)
Devotions from the World of Music
  Ages 8+ (David C. Cook/Chariot Victor)
Devotions from the World of Women's Sports
  Ages 8+ (David C. Cook/Chariot Victor)

BIBLE STORY CD-ROMS
The Beginners Bible Series
  Ages 3-8 (Baker)
My 100 All-Time Favorite Bible Stories
  Ages 5-8 (Baker)
The Birth of Jesus Activity Center
  Ages 0-4 (Baker)
Interactive Bible for Kids Series
  Ages 3-8 (Tyndale)
The Treasure Study Bible
  Ages 7+ (Kirkbride)
Children's Bible – 140 Stories
  Ages 4+ (Heaven Word)
Read With Me Bible
  Ages 5-10 (Zondervan)
Noah & The Ark, Jonah & the Whale – A Play Along Storybook
  Ages 3-8 (Parsons)

Children's Activity Bible
   Ages 2+ (Thomas Nelson)
My Play Time Friends
   Ages 3+ (Standard)
God Loves Me
   Ages 3+ (Standard)
God's A-Z Creatures
   Ages 3+ (Standard)
Heroes of the Bible
   Ages 3+ (Standard)
Time Travelers Explore the Bible
   Ages 3+ (Standard)

MAGAZINES
Clubhouse Jr.
   Ages 4-8 (Focus on the Family)
Clubhouse
   Ages 8-12 (Focus on the Family)

BIBLE STORY BOOKS
Baby Bible
   Ages 1-3 (Chariot Victor)
The Beginners Bible
   Ages 3-8 (Zondervan)
The Children's Bible Story Book
   Ages 3-8 (Thomas Nelson)
The Bible in Pictures for Little Eyes
   Ages 3-7 (Moody)
Read With Me Bible
   Ages 4-8 (Zondervan)
The Children's Bible in 365 Stories
   Ages 8-12 (Lion Publishing)
Hurlburt's Story of the Bible
   All ages (Zondervan)
Little Girls Bible Storybook for Mothers & Daughters
   Ages 4-7 (Baker)
God's Story
   Ages 5-8 (Tyndale)

The Amazing Treasure Bible
    Ages 6-12 (Zondervan)
The Rhyme Bible Story Book
    Ages 3-8 (Zondervan)
The Beginners Bible
    Ages 2-6
The Children's Discovery Bible
    Ages 3-6 (Chariot Victor)
The Praise Bible
    Ages 2-6 (WaterBrook)
My First Bible in Pictures
    Ages Birth–3 (Tyndale)
ABC Bible Storybook
    Ages 4-7 (Chariot Victor)

BIOGRAPHIES
Billy Sunday
Billy Graham
Corrie Ten Boom
David Brainerd
Hudson Taylor
Jim Elliot
Luis Palau
Borden of Yale
C.S. Lewis
Mary Slessor
Eric Liddell
John and Betty Stam

CHARACTER BUILDING BOOKS
Uncle Arthur's Bedtime Stories Classics, Vol. 1-5
    Out of Print
A Child's First Steps to Virtue
    Ages 3-8 (Harvest House)
The Children's Book of Virtues
    Ages 4-8 (Simon & Schuster)

CHARACTER BUILDING TAPES & CDS
24 Dramatized Bible Stories on 12 Cassettes
    Ages 3-10 (Christian Duplications)

Fill Up On God's Word – Bible Truths for Children in 12 Tapes
   Ages 3-10 (Christian Duplications)
The Easter Lily – Tape & Book
   (Brentwood – Benson)
Bible Stories for the Family Series
   (Simitar Entertainment)
Mark Lowry's Cassette and Book Series
   Ages 2-10 (Gaither Collections)
Adventures in Odyssey Series
   Ages 8+ (Focus on the Family)

CHARACTER BUILDING VIDEO TAPES
McGee and Me Series
   Ages 5-15 (Focus on the Family)
Adventures in Odyssey Series
   Ages 8+ (Focus on the Family)
Quigley's Village Series
   Ages 2-7 (Zondervan)
The Donut Man Series
   Ages 2-8 (Integrity Music)
The Chronicles of Narnia Series
   All ages (Zondervan)
Veggie Tales Series
   (Word)
The Simple Grand Quigley Band Series
   Ages 2-7 (Zondervan)
Bibleman Series
   Ages 3-9 (Pamplin)
Kingdom Adventure Series
   Out of Print
Fabulicious Day Series
   Ages 2-6 (Chariot Victor)
Guidepost's Junction – True Stories to Help Build Character
   Ages 5-10 (Sparrow)
Adventures from the Book of Virtues
   (Porch Light Entertainment)

SURVEY MATERIAL
Search Institute, 700 South Third St., Suite 210, Minneapolis, MN 55415
   (Toll Free Phone, 1 (800) 888-7828) www.search-institute.org

SCIENCE & THE BIBLE VIDEOS
Newton's Workshop Series
Ages 4+ (Moody)

PRAYER VIDEOS
Time to Pray: The Adventures of Prayer Bear, Vol. 1-3
Ages 5-10 (Sparrow)

BIBLE STORY VIDEOS
The Beginners Bible Series
(Word)
The Storykeepers Series
Ages 6-12 (Zondervan)
Superbook Video Bible Series
Ages 2+ (Tyndale)

MUSIC VIDEOS
Kids Sing Praise Series
(Brentwood – Benson)
Hide 'Em In Your Heart Series
Ages 5-10 (Sparrow)
Cedarmont Kids Series
(Brentwood – Benson)
Psalty's Series
(Word)
Gaither Kids Series
Ages 2-10 (Gaither Collection)
25 Bible Action Songs Kids Love to Sing
(Straightway)
My First Hymnal
Ages 2-8 (Henley Productions)

MUSIC CDS
Hide 'Em In Your Heart, Vol. 1-3
Ages 5-10 (Sparrow)
Cedarmont Kids Series
(Brentwood – Benson)
Psalty's Series
(Word)

My First Hymnal
  Ages 2-8 (Henley Productions)
Kids Sing Praise Series
  (Brentwood – Benson)
America's 25 Favorite Praise & Worship Choruses for Kids
  (Brentwood – Benson)
Angels All Around Series
  (Word)
Songfest, Vol. 1-2
  (Chariot Victor)
Great Songs for Kids Series
  (Word)
The Beginners Bible Songs for Young Children
  Ages 5-11 (Rhino Records)
Heaven's Sake Kids
  (Sparrow)
Cedarmont Kids Series
  (Brentwood – Benson)
Kids' Collection Series
  (Brentwood – Benson)
Kids on the Rock
  Ages 6-8 (Gospel Light)
Veggie Tales Series – With Book
  Ages 3+ (Word)
Sunday School Favorites Series
  (Word)

ACTIVITY BOOKS
Bible Time Crafts Your Kids Will Love
  Ages 6-12 (Group)
Forget-Me-Not Bible Story Activities
  Ages 6-12 (Group)
More Than Mud Pies – Bible Learning Crafts & Games for Preschoolers
  (Group)
The Big Book of Bible Games
  Ages 6-12 (Gospel Light)
Nature Crafts for Children
  Ages 3+ (Baker)

Family Night Tool Chest Series
    Family (Chariot Victor)
Value Builders Series
    Ages 6-12 (David C. Cook/ Chariot Victor)
Crafts and More
    Ages 6-12 (Group)
Parties With A Purpose
    Ages 2-15 (Thomas Nelson)
Party! Party!
    Ages 6-12 (Group)
Old Testament/New Testament Activity Bible
    (Hunt & Thorpe)

QUESTION AND ANSWER BOOKS
The Wonder Book – Answers to Kids Questions
    Ages 5-8 (Child Evangelism)
The Big Book of Questions and Answers
    (Christian Focus Publications)
What is God Like?
    Ages 3-6 (Tyndale)

GAME CDS
Bible Baseball
    Ages 5-8 (Baker)
Bible Coloring Book
    Ages 5-8 (Baker)
Bible Activities on CD-ROM
    Ages 5-8 (Baker)
My First Bible Games
    Ages 4-8 (Chariot Victor)
Ultimate Bible Games Series
    All ages (Logos Productions)
Bible Time Fun
    Ages 4-12 (Bridgestone Multimedia Group)
Family Bible Game Collection on 5 CD-ROMs
    Ages 7+ (Good News Software)

FAMILY GAMES

Kids Bible Challenge
 Ages 6-12 (Chariot Victor)
Life Stories. . .Remember the Time
 Ages 8-Adult (Standard)
Kids Choices
 Ages 6-12 (Chariot Victor)
Noah's Memory Match-Up Game
 Ages 3+ (Chariot Victor)
WWJD –What Would Jesus Do? – The Game
 Ages teen+ (Cadaco)
The Game of Scattergories–Bible Edition
 Ages 8+ (Cactus)
Redemption – A Collectible Trading Card Game Based on the Bible Ages 9+
 (Cactus)
Bible Treasure Hunt
 Ages 10+ (Standard)
Jacob's Ladder
 Ages 8-12 (Standard)
Bibleopoly
 Ages 8+ (Late for the Sky)
Money Matters for Kids
 Ages 5-10 (Chariot Victor)
Kids Bible Challenge
 Ages 6-12 (Chariot Victor)
Bible Scrabble
 Ages 10+ (Review & Herald Publishing)
Journey Through Bible Land
 Ages 3-6 (Chariot Victor)
Glory
 Ages 5+ (Grace Publications)
Noah's Ark Memory Match
 Ages 3+ (Grace Publications)
Bible Stories Sorting and Matching Game
 Ages 4+ (Grace Publications)
Bible Categories
 Ages 12+ (Chariot Victor)

Bible Challenge
   Ages 10+ (Chariot Victor)
Bible Charades
   Ages 10+ (Chariot Victor)
Sticky Situations – McGee & Me Game
   Ages 6+ (Tyndale)

PUBLISHERS

Baker Book House/Revell, P. O. Box 6287, Grand Rapids, MI 49516 (800) 877-2665
Barbour Publishing, Inc., Box 719, Uhrichsville, OH 44683 (740) 922-6045
Brentwood-Benson Music, 365 Great Circle Road, Nashville, TN 37228
   (800) 333-9000
Bridgestone Multimedia Group, 300 N. McKemy Ave., Chandler, AZ 85226
   (602) 940-5777
Broadman & Holman Publishers, 127 Ninth Ave. N., Nashville, TN 37234
   (800) 725-5416
Cactus Game Design, 1553 S. Military Hwy., Chesapeake, VA 23320 (800) 365-1711
Cadaco, 4300 W. 47th St., Chicago, IL 60632 (773) 927-1500
Chariot Victor Publishing, 4050 Lee Vance View, Colorado Springs, CO 80918
   (800) 437-4337
Child Evangelism Fellowship, P. O. Box 348, Warrenton, MO 63383 (314) 456-4321
Christian Duplications Int'l, 1710 Lee Road, Orlando, FL 32810 (407) 298-6612
Christian Educational Services, 11911 McIntosh Road, Thonotosassa, FL 33592
   (813) 986-4761
Concordia Publishing House, 3558 S. Jefferson Ave., St. Louis, MO 63118
   (800) 325-3040
David C. Cook/Chariot Victor, 4050 Lee Vance View, Colorado Springs, CO 80918
   (719) 536-0100
Discovery House Publishers, P. O. Box 3566, Grand Rapids, MI 49501
   (800) 653-8333
Focus on the Family, 8605 Explorer Dr., Colorado Springs, CO 80920
   (719) 531-3496
Gaither Collection, Box 178, Alexandria, IN 46001 (800) 955-8746
Good News Software, 1300 Crescent St., Wheaton, IL 60187 (630) 682-4300
Gospel Light/Regal Books, 2300 Knoll Dr., Ventura, CA 93003 (805) 644-9721
Grace Publications, 23740 Hawthorne Blvd., Torrance, CA 90505 (310) 378-1133
Group Publishing, Inc., 1515 Cascade Ave., Loveland, CO 80538 (970) 669-3836
Harper Collins Publishers, 10 E. 53rd St., New York, NY 10022 (212) 207-7000
Harvest House Publishers, 1075 Arrowsmith, Eugene, OR 97402 (541) 343-0123
Heaven Word, 2940 Trawick Road, #9, Raleigh, NC 27604 (919) 876-1124
Henly Productions, Box 40269, Nashville, TN 37204 (615) 383-8845
Ideal/Instructional Fair, Box 1650, Grand Rapids, MI 49501 (800) 633-4606
Immigration and Refugee Service, 1717 Mass. Ave. NW, Ste. 701, Washington, D.C.
   20036 (202) 797-2105

Integrity Music Co., 1050 5th Ave., #14A, New York, NY 10028 (212) 348-3990
Kirkbride Bible Company, Box 606, Indianapolis, IN 46206 (800) 428-4385
Legacy Press, P. O. box 261129, San Diego, CA 92196 (619) 578-1273
Lion Publishing, Peter's Way, Sandy Lane West, Oxford OX4 5HG
    UNITED KINGDOM 011-441-865-747550
Logos Productions Inc., 6160 Carman Ave. E., Inver Grove Heights, MN 5076
    (800) 875-6467
Maher Studios, Box 420, Littleton, CO 80160 (303) 798-6830
Moody Press, 820 N. LaSalle Dr., Chicago, IL 60610 (800) 678-8812
Multnomah Publishers, P. O. Box 1720, Sisters, OR 97759 (800) 929-0910
NavPress Publishing Group, 7899 Lexington Dr., Colorado Springs, CO 80920
    (800) 366-7788
Off the Curb Publishing, 306-N West El Norte Parkway, Suite 352, Escondido, CA
    92026 (760) 738-7039
One Way Street, P. O. Box 5077, Englewood, CO 80155 (303) 790-1188
Pamplin Music Corp., 10209 SE Division St., Portland, OR 97266 (503) 251-1555
Parson's Technology, Box 100, Hiawatha, IA 52233 (319) 395-9626
Porch Light Entertainment, 11828 LaGrange Ave., Los Angeles, CA 90025
    (310) 477-8400
Puppet Factory, 117 E. 17th St., Goodland, KS 67735 (785) 899-7143
Review & Herald Publishing, 55 W. Oak Ridge Dr., Hagerstown, MD 21740
    (301) 791-7000
Rhino Records, 10635 Santa Monica Blvd., Los Angeles, CA 90025 (310) 474-4778
Simitar Entertainment, Inc., 5555 Pioneer Creek Dr., Maple Plain, MN 55359
    (612) 479-7000
Simon & Schuster, 1230 Avenue of the Americas, New York, NY 10020
    (800) 223-2336
Son Shine Puppet Co., P. O. Box 6203, Rockford, IL 61125 (815) 965-8080
Sparrow Corporation, P. O. Box 5010, Brentwood, TN 37024 (615) 371-6800
Standard Publishing, 8121 Hamilton Ave., Cincinnati, OH 45231 (800) 542-1301
Straightway, Inc., Box 74068, Romulus, MI 48174 (734) 946-2108
Thomas Nelson Publishing, 501 Nelson Place, Nashville, TN 37214 (800) 251-4000
Tyndale House Publishers, P. O. Box 80, Wheaton, IL 60189 (800) 323-9400
Walk Thru the Bible, 4201 N. Peachtree Rd., Atlanta, GA 30341 (770) 458-9300
WaterBrook Press, 5446 N. Academy Blvd., #200, Colorado Springs, CO 80918
    (719) 590-4999
Word Entertainment, Box 141000, Nashville, TN 37214 (888) 324-9673
World Relief Corporation, P. O. Box WRC, Nyack, NY 10960 (914) 268-4135
World Vision, Box 9716, Federal Way, WA 98063 (253) 815-1000
Zondervan Publishing House, 5300 Patterson Ave. SE, Grand Rapids, MI 49530
    (800) 727-1309

Idea Index

Idea Index

Endnotes

CHAPTER 1

1 J. Otis Ledbetter and Kurt Bruner, *Your Heritage* (Colorado Springs, CO: Chariot Victor Publishing, 1999) 27.
2 Ledbetter, *Your Heritage*, 60.
3 Ledbetter, *Your Heritage*, 77.
4 *Noah Webster's 1828 Dictionary* (Anaheim, CA: Foundation for American Christian Education, 1967)
5 *Noah Webster's 1828 Dictionary*

CHAPTER 2

1 Lisa F. Berkman, *Health and Ways of Living: the Alameda Study* (New York, NY: Oxford Press, 1983).
2 Edward Hallowell, *Connect* (New York, NY: Pantheon, a division of Random House, 1999) 3.
3 Craig Hill, *Bar Barakah* (Littleton, CO: Family Foundational Int., 1998) 8.
4 Zig Ziglar as quoted in Kendra Smiley, *Empowered by Choice* (Ann Arbor, Michigan: Servant, 1998) 145.
5 As quoted in Kendra Smiley, *Empowered by Choice*, 159.

CHAPTER 3

1 "Clips," *New Man*, Nov-Dec. 1994.
2 Jeff Bridges, *Parade*, quoted in *Readers' Digest*, Jan. 1996.

3 Muhammad Ali, *Readers' Digest*, Feb, 1996.
4 A. Proulx, as quoted in Current Biography, *Readers' Digest*,
   Jan. 1996.

CHAPTER 4

1 Patrick Morley, *Walking with Christ in the Details of Life*
   (Nashville: Thomas Nelson, 1998) as quoted in New Man
   (March-April, 1995).
2 Eric Berne, *Games People Play* (New York: Valentine Books,
   1996).
3 C.S. Lewis, *The Weight of Glory and Other Addresses* (New York:
   Macmillan, 1980), 18-19.

CHAPTER 5

1 Gary Smalley and John Trent, *The Blessing* (Nashville: Nelson,
   1986) 40-41.
2 For more ideas on this subject, we recommend J. Otis and
   Gail Ledbetter, *Family Fragrance* (Colorado Springs, CO:
   Chariot Victor Publishing, 1998).
3 For more about true north, we recommend Kurt and Olivia
   Bruner, *Family Compass* (Colorado Springs, CO: Chariot Victor
   Publishing, 1999).
4 For a more in-depth study of traditions and their value, we
   recommend J. Otis Ledbetter and Tim Smith, *Family Traditions*
   (Colorado Springs, CO: Chariot Victor Publishing, 1998).
5 For great information and activities we recommend Jim
   Weidmann and Kurt Bruner, *Family Night Tool Chests 1-10*
   (Colorado Springs, CO: Chariot Victor Publishing, 1997, 1998,
   1999, 2000).
6 Ledbetter and Bruner, *Your Heritage*, 197.

CHAPTER 6

1 Charles Swindoll, *The Strong Family* (Anaheim, CA: Insight
   for Living, 1991) 10.
2 Search Institute; Copyright © 1997 by Search Institute, 700 5.
   Third Street, Suite 210, Minneapolis, MN 55415; 800-888-7828.
   This list may be reproduced for educational, noncommercial

uses solely. Copyright © 1997 by Search Institute, 700 5. Third
Street, Suite 210, Minneapolis, MN 55415; 800-888-7828.

3 Ibid.

CHAPTER 7

1 Ledbetter and Bruner, *Your Heritage*, 197.